Religion and Faith in Latin America

RELIGION AND FAITH IN LATIN AMERICA

W. STANLEY RYCROFT

With a Foreword by Alberto Rembao

Philadelphia
THE WESTMINSTER PRESS

© W. L. JENKINS MCMLVIII

Library of Congress Catalog Card No. 58–5838

PRINTED IN THE UNITED STATES OF AMERICA

Contents

Foreword

This volume is different from most on the Latin American theme. Rising above the similarity of ideas and repetition of facts to be found in most treatises on the subject, this book is different in that it has form — or rather is " in form." To be " in form " is to have rhythm, as on the athletic field, so that when one falls he lands on his feet. Ideas become sterile and facts obsolete unless they are " in-formed " and enlivened. The ideas of RELIGION AND FAITH IN LATIN AMERICA are saved from the inanity of the commonplace, and its facts transcend the rigor of mere statistics, because the fact appears tinged with personal experience and the idea inflamed by an ardent passion.

Our author knows his Latin America, as could be expected of the traveler and scholar that he is; but here knowledge serves a higher meaning, enlightened by the feeling for a Latin America that has become bone of his bones and flesh of his flesh. His postgraduate academic training was Hispanic, he once heard the Macedonian call to pass over into Peru to help the brethren, and his life career has been that of a missionary. No wonder, then, that his knowledge attains another quality, since it seems to be subordinated to his theme, Latin America. This theme takes possession of our author's pen like a living presence and a compelling reality.

Furthermore, this book renders a valuable service to all who would know Latin America in order to understand it and love it. It appears at a very opportune moment, when the heretofore opaque Protestant aspect of the Green Continent is coming into

7

the noonday light; when everyone must take notice of the Protestant factor as a demographic quantum, as a democratic ingredient, and as a cultural asset. The visible sociological phenomenon is that a new community has been born in the midst of the old one. The Reformation has appeared in Hispanic dress; there has been a new birth of religious consciousness affecting the daily life of millions of people. The spiritual élan that four centuries ago was suffocated at the stake in Valladolid and Seville emerges now triumphant in the "American Spains."

Protestant Christianity south of the Rio Grande is a product of the soil, for the spearhead and the bulk and the spirit of the Evangelical movement are "native." And since this is so, the missionary effort from abroad has been nothing more than a catalytic destined to activate the movement of history under God. In fact, Hispanic Protestantism has reached such stages of vitality and potency that even the spokesmen of the established church are calling upon their faithful not to attack, nor to refute, nor to stop the Protestant wave, but rather to excel or outdo it. They see in its life and work "a lesson in methodology," and in its lay members sincere, convinced militant propagators, who at the moment have already altered the religious world view in their lands.

To be sure, this tribute reveals a force in action that, in due season, may also affect the character and quality of Christianity in other countries. This new Hispanic Reformation is contagious. As a contemporary version of Hispanic individualism, it has found a modern application for the doctrine of the "priesthood of all believers," which, in Latin America, can be expressed in the slogan, "every believer a preacher." Laymen have taken unto themselves holy orders, so to speak, according to the rite of Melchizedek; and the gospel is seen to operate like nascent hydrogen. The Evangelical communities of the Caribbean Isles and the Andean slopes and the crowded metropolises of the Amazon and River Plate areas become truly the salt of the earth and the light of the world.

ALBERTO REMBAO

Preface

All through history man has practiced religious forms and rituals, performed ceremonies, and offered sacrifices in an attempt to placate or to please his various deities and induce them to serve his purposes. Religion offers man the line of least resistance, for it is admittedly easier to comply with the requirements of a religious system than to meet the demands of a faith such as the Christian, involving fidelity to high ideals and ethical principles.

Latin America's great need is not for more religion, but for a vital, dynamic faith that not only transforms men morally and spiritually but sends them forth to challenge evils and injustices, remaking society through the concerted action and penetrating influence of the church of Jesus Christ.

The extraordinary development of the Evangelical movement in Latin America in recent years contains the promise of a new day; however, it also raises many problems and creates new situations calling for vision and long-range planning. The leaders of the Evangelical churches, as well as the rank and file, are challenged as never before to witness to the realities of the Christian faith and to serve their day and generation.

The reader will not find in this book a description of Protestant work in Latin America. That can be found elsewhere. We have endeavored to show the relative sterility of religion as compared with a vital Christian faith encompassing the whole of life.

Latin America today is a battlefield for men's minds in the midst of a social revolution. These are crucial times, when humanity is on the march, seeking new ways to solve old problems, and the task is a compelling one. Christianity, with its emphasis on the worth and dignity of the individual and the freedom of the human spirit under the discipline of God, is the surest foundation of the liberty and democracy for which Latin America yearns. Thus we believe that the Christian gospel is the answer to the deepest problems of Latin American life and culture today. However, that answer can be given only if the Evangelical churches are willing to use all their resources and press forward as members of the body of Christ in a courageous and vital encounter with the world.

The author wishes to express his indebtedness to the many persons who have contributed, directly or indirectly, in the preparation of this book.

Indirect help has come from the rich and varied sources of information that are available in English, Spanish, and Portuguese on the Latin American theme, and from these he has drawn freely.

Direct and valuable aid has been given by those friends who have sustained him in the task, with their unfailing encouragement, and by those who were willing to give the necessary time to read the preliminary draft of the manuscript and make important suggestions regarding changes.

To the author's wife, without whose painstaking collaboration this book would not have been possible, also goes his deepest appreciation.

W. Stanley Rycroft

I

Ideological Mainstreams

This book is devoted to a study of the nature and influence of religion in Latin America today, and the need for a dynamic Christian faith. It should be borne in mind that the terms "religion" and "faith" are not synonymous and that we have made a fundamental differentiation between the two. As an ecclesiastical system and a set of observances, religion can have a repressive effect on a people, contributing very little, if anything, to individual development or social progress. Faith, on the other hand, is the fountainhead from which springs the continuous flow of life-giving energy which nourishes and vitalizes all aspects of existence. The future of Latin America may well be determined by the extent to which a living, creative Christian faith is able to capture the soul of its people.

In analyzing the forces that contribute to making a people what it is, we find a complex interplay of racial and ethnic factors, the influence of geographic position, topography, natural wealth, social and economic development, psychological characteristics, and political history. Consideration will be given to these as they have helped to mold the Latin American people and have influenced directions and trends.

Important as these factors are in determining the destiny of nations, they play secondary roles to the impact of ideologies in effecting that determination, for all history is, in essence, a history of ideas. Vigorous, progressive ideas are the mainsprings of action, prompting a people to form democratic institutions and to be creative and productive; stultifying ideas are like stagnant pools wherein perish all aspirations and hopes for a better society. It is because we believe so firmly in the power of ideas to activate or to inhibit that we have undertaken the present study.

Religious ideas in particular are potent in affecting norms of living, behavior and culture patterns. The religious history of Latin America may be divided into three broad periods: (1) the pre-Columbian religions of the Mayas, Aztecs, and Incas; (2) Roman Catholicism as the dominant religion; and (3) the advent of Protestantism or Evangelical Christianity. We shall attempt to deal with this religious heritage of the Latin American people, showing how basic it is to the understanding of their way of life. The cultural mores and thought patterns of Latin America are outstandingly Roman Catholic, and the social and economic orbit within which it moves has the imprint of the Church of Rome. Without a doubt the most important ideological influence on the Latin American scene has been that of Roman Catholicism. We share the view of Richard Pattee, leading Roman Catholic layman, when he says, " Latin America is what it is because Catholicism is what it is." [1] It is therefore imperative that we understand something of the historic events that influenced the type of religion that crossed the Atlantic Ocean in the sixteenth century to establish itself in the New World.

THE RENAISSANCE AND THE REFORMATION

Two movements that took shape in the fifteenth century in Europe and profoundly altered the course of history were the Renaissance and the Reformation. They represented not only the transition from the Middle Ages to the modern era, but also, in the realm of the spirit, gave rise to an age of adventure and set in motion many forces that were to mold Western civilization.

While we shall point out some of the distinctive features of these movements, it must be recognized that there was a parallel development and, in some areas, much overlapping of the two. Some of the Reformers were Humanists, as the men of the Renaissance were called, and some of the Humanists were Reformers.

Both movements were, in a sense, a revolt against the accepted concepts, standards, and values of the Middle Ages and both challenged medieval authority, although the challenge took different forms. They transmuted into thought and action the inevitable breakup of the old order and the general feeling of unrest of the times.

The need to reform or to revolt becomes imperative when the gap between the external order and accepted standards of morality and justice grows too wide. The Middle Ages had become intolerable to many because there was such a great discrepancy between the ideal and the real. The Christian promise was one of peace, security, and brotherhood; the reality was in sharp contrast. It was an indecent scramble for power, position, and wealth, in a stratified world based on feudalism, where the poor were not only abysmally poor, but ignorant and half starved. The cleavage between the promise and the fulfillment had become unbearable. " Shocked by the gulf between theory and practice," says R. H. Tawney, " men turned this way and that to find some solution of the tension which racked them. The German Reformers followed one road and preached a return to primitive simplicity. . . . The Humanists took another, which should lead to the gradual regeneration of mankind by the victory of reason over superstition and avarice." [2]

Men looked in vain to the church of that day for an example of Christian conduct and practice. Tawney also says: "Its [the church's] teaching was violated in practice, and violated grossly, in the very citadel of Christendom which promulgated it. . . . From the middle of the thirteenth century, a continuous wail arises against the iniquity of the church, and its burden may be summed up in one word, ' avarice.' At Rome everything is for sale." [3]

The Renaissance which developed principally, though not wholly, in the Latin countries of Europe, while it was a revolt against medieval forms and values, was able to flourish under the aegis of the Roman Church and left its structure intact and its authority unshaken. The Reformation, on the other hand, developed in the northern part of Europe. It created a schism within the church and drew several countries away from its religious and political hegemony.

While the Reformation was largely a spiritual movement, the Renaissance was related to learning and knowledge. The Humanists were scholars, men of letters, scientists, philosophers, and political theorists. In their revolt against medieval habits of mind, and in their rejection of outmoded thought forms, particularly those imposed by the scholasticism of the times, these men of the Renaissance turned to the classical period of Greece and Rome and drew upon those pagan sources for their inspiration. It is not suprising that many Humanists had a thorough knowledge of Latin and Greek, which gave them access to the literary, scientific, and philosophical treasures of the past. There was also a new interest in geographic knowledge and discovery as the borders of the known world began to recede. The printing press became an invaluable tool, which enabled the Humanists to communicate their ideas as their predecessors had not been able to do.

Most of the Humanists were a privileged group of learned men who were vitally interested in knowledge for its own sake and very proud of their scholarly attainments, largely academic in outlook, and detached from the common man and his needs. They neither were crusaders for great causes nor did they evince much interest in spreading knowledge and learning among the people; they produced an intellectual elite. They had little or no effect on improving the low moral tone of their time.

The revival of all forms of art and literature — and also scientific discoveries — which flourished during the period of the Renaissance and had tremendous influence on our civilization, while it broke the old molds that had incarcerated previous generations within the narrow confines of prescribed norms and patterns, might be said to have made its greatest impact on the secular aspects of culture. Theological preoccupations and speculations were not within the province of the Humanists as a whole. Therefore, the supremacy of the church in Latin countries came through unscathed, and its authority was virtually unshaken. In fact, some of the concepts held by the men of the Renaissance intensified the power of the church and further built up its authoritarianism. The realms of politics and ecclesiasticism were touching at most points in medieval Europe; the Humanists' stanch belief in the principle of absolute monarchy strengthened the hand of tyrants, and their upholding of the " divine right of kings " equated the temporal power of the monarch with the heavenly connections of the church.

Throughout the Middle Ages, both in Spain and in Italy, there had been some degree of democracy — sporadic, perhaps, but alive. The absolute authority of a king was being challenged in Spain at about the time the barons were facing John at Runnymede. Many other attempts were made at obtaining individual liberties. One such effort in Spain was as early as the seventh century, when the famous *Fuero Juzgo* stated that " the peoples were not made for kings, but kings for the peoples, nor did the kings create the peoples but the peoples made the kings." The revival of pagan political concepts of authoritarian rule which came out of the Renaissance, and the widespread acceptance of these, finally succeeded in snuffing out the enfeebled rays of democratic strivings in the Latin countries, especially the Iberian peninsula.

It is important to remember, too, that ancient pagan customs, ideas, and superstitions never entirely disappeared in the Latin countries of Europe such as Italy, France, Spain, and Portugal, for while it is true they were considered to be Christian lands, nevertheless Christianity had compromised with pagan thought, belief, and practice. "Ancient paganism [in these lands], in truth, has never died. It still lives and appears in many superstitions, too numerous to be mentioned in detail, in many customs and sentiments which either never existed in the countries of the north or were banished and came to be pure fables, with no influence. The reason is that since the ancient paganism in those lands had no Homer to sing its praises nor a Phidias who by materializing it glorified it, it never took such deep root nor became strong. In the Latin countries it has always existed and, as is abundantly proved by the literature and art of the nineteenth century, there is always the danger that the ancient gods may be resurrected. This was precisely the value and deep significance of the Renaissance, that powerful current which slew venerable institutions, both democratic and Christian, which the Latin peoples had been able to set up in Europe during the Middle Ages." [4]

Let us now turn to a consideration of the Reformation; it too was a revolt against the authority of the Middle Ages, and a reaction to the moral and spiritual decadence of the period.

The Reformation has sometimes been regarded as a protest, a breaking away from the Christian church, a sort of reckless adventure, at best an innovation. The Reformers, however, maintained that they were restoring rather than innovating, *reforming* instead of creating. Whereas the Humanists went back to classical pagan sources for their inspiration in art, literature, science, and politics, and were in the stream of the Greco-Roman tradition, the Reformers, brushing aside all the accretions which had been assimilated into the Christian church through contact with pagan religions and through the corruption and deterioration of centuries, returned to the original source of Christianity, the New Testament, and sought as well to bring their thinking into line with the Hebrew traditions of justice, spirituality, and monotheism, as expressed in the Old Testament. In the New Testament they found, not only the narrative of the life of Christ, his teachings, his example, his death and resurrection, but also the doctrines, beliefs, and practices of the early Christian church.

It is important to remember that the outcome of the conflict between Roman Catholicism and the sixteenth-century Reformers went beyond matters of doctrine and theology. The socio-politico-economic implications latent in the Reformation were so far-reaching in their consequences that they shook the whole structure of the Roman Church to its foundations.

The Reformation was far more revolutionary even in an ideological sense than the Reformers themselves realized. Individual freedom, freedom of conscience, freedom of interpretation (which is the basis of modern science), religious freedom, and a personal relationship with God — all these were implicit in the change of direction brought about by the Reformation. The Reformers were not at first fully aware of the tremendous consequences of their actions in challenging medieval ecclesiastical authority and rediscovering the foundations of the Christian faith.

The Reformation made rapid strides in northern Europe; it took such deep root because the discovery of the printing press made it possible to bring translations of the Bible in the vernacular within reach of the common man. Until that time only those who knew Latin, Greek, or Hebrew could read the Scriptures and thus the ordinary person had access to them only through the priests. The Reformers established schools and gave great impetus to popular education, a fact which is of profound significance in the development of democracy.

THE SPANISH REFORMATION THAT FAILED

As we are dealing specifically with the long-range effects of these two great historical movements — the Renaissance and the Reformation — on Latin America, and as the predominant religion there is the Roman Catholicism that came from Spain, we will now turn to a consideration of the development of Christianity in that country.

When did Christianity first reach the Iberian shores? Tradition has it that the beginnings of Christianity in Spain go back to the times of the apostles themselves, though there is some doubt as to whether Paul was the first messenger of the gospel, or James. There is some historical support for the belief that Paul visited Spain in the course of his missionary journeys, but the tradition making James the first Christian to visit the country seems to have had more popular support. " The history of Spain," says Américo Castro, " cannot be understood without a knowledge and understanding of the veneration paid to Saint James the Apostle. . . . Faith in the physical presence of the apostle gave spiritual support to those who fought against the Moors." [5] It is interesting to note that Castro devotes seventy pages in his monumental book on Spain to a consideration of the belief in Saint

James of Galicia, and to the decline in that veneration, which took place in the seventeenth century.

Be this as it may, the Christian church that was established in Spain in the early days was very different from the type of Roman Catholicism that was later taken to the New World. Its form was simple and pure; there were no pictures or images in places of worship, and only two sacraments were observed, Baptism and Communion. All members partook of the bread and wine during the administration of Communion. Beginning with the third century, however, accretions began to appear, and these multiplied as time went on. For instance, accommodations were made to pagan practices such as the use of incense, and the introduction of holy water for the sprinkling and blessing of the faithful. Worship became the Mass, prayers were offered to the saints, the celibacy of the priesthood was instituted, and penance and monastic life were established.

As early as the fourth century, men of faith began to rebel against these impurities and corruptions and advocate a return to primitive forms of Christianity. The first Spanish voice that was raised against the Church of Rome because of the growing tendency to absorb pagan practices was that of Prisciliano, who was martyred in A.D. 385. He wrote a concordance of Paul's epistles and it was he who first divided the Bible into chapters and verses. He was a vigorous defender of the principle of private interpretation, later to be enunciated by the Reformers of the sixteenth century. His faith was Christ-centered, and can be summed up in his own words: "For us, to live is Christ, and life is Christ, and faith is Christ." [6]

During the centuries that followed, many were those who challenged the impious practices of the church, and some of them suffered cruel martyrdom because of their undeviating allegiance to the Christian ideal and their desire to keep its pristine purity uncontaminated. The history books tell the story of these men who unflinchingly met their fate rather than temporize on matters of faith and practice.

The Reformation burst upon the northern countries of Europe

in the early years of the sixteenth century. Its strength lay not only in such eminent figures as Zwingli, Luther, and Calvin, but in the Bible as the Word of God. Persecution on the part of the Roman Church was directed not just against dissenters; there was vigorous opposition to the translation of the Scriptures into the language of the people.

Spain also felt the influence of the Reformation. Around the year 1521 Protestant tracts and pamphlets began to enter the country and were read avidly by many people. The authorities burned as many of these publications as they could lay hands on, but others were read and passed around, and they had an effect on the minds and spirits of the readers. The first Protestant congregation to be established was in Seville, and its first pastor was a doctor of medicine named Cristóbal Losada. It was called by the significant name of Templo de la Nueva Luz (Temple of New Light). At one time it had about a thousand members. They met clandestinely once or twice a week in a private house. The membership was drawn largely from among the educated classes — doctors, writers, lawyers, and army officers — and included a few members of the nobility. In 1559 the existence and whereabouts of the congregation became known to the Inquisition authorities, and eight hundred of the members were thrown into prison prior to being brought before that dread tribunal. Sixty persons were sentenced to be strangled and at least twenty were sentenced to death by fire. Shortly afterward, the prior and many of the friars of the monastery of San Isidro, near Seville, were converted to the new faith, possibly through the influence of the literature that still came from abroad, or by contact with some members of the ill-fated Seville congregation. When they were discovered, some friars were able to flee the country, but most of them, among whom was the prior, were tried and sentenced to be burned alive.

In addition to the above examples, there were other groups and congregations in various Spanish cities that strove to keep alive the real spirit of Christianity amid the encroaching and ever-growing agglomeration of extraneous practices and doctrines that were being incorporated into the ritual and the dogmas of the church.

The Inquisition achieved success in its work of tracking down all who were even suspected of embracing the Reformed faith. All who could do so fled across the borders, where they continued to worship according to their conscience, associating themselves with other congregations, or establishing groups of religious exiles in other countries. Thus Juan Pérez de Pineda, a theologian and former diplomat, became the pastor of a Spanish congregation in Geneva and began work on a Spanish translation of the Bible. He sent his incomplete work to Casiodoro de Reina, who, after nearly twelve years of intensive and incessant labor, published the first complete Bible in Spanish in the city of Basel in 1569. Years later, as a continuation of Casiodoro's work, Cipriano de Valera brought out his translation in 1599. This translation, known as the Valera, is still in use in many parts of the Spanish world.[7]

We have cited only a few examples to show the nature of the Reformation movement in Spain. The interesting point to remember is that this Reformation was a reality, and not only that, but it was entirely Spanish in character. The churches, pastors, and workers were Spaniards; only the stimulus came from abroad. Many of the leaders of the movement were bishops, priests, and friars within the Roman Catholic Church, and its lay leaders were able men and women from the better classes. "Some of Spain's best minds in the realms of religion and culture in the golden age of Spanish literature were either Protestants or sympathizers with the new ideas. . . . One Spanish historian goes so far as to say that the Protestant influence and trend in the sixteenth century were so strong that, if the Inquisition had delayed its activities for only a few months, the country might well have become Protestant."[8]

Erasmus, one of the outstanding Humanists, and a bridge between the Renaissance and the Reformation, had many followers in Spain. He believed that a true reformation should begin with a translation of the Word of God which could be put into the hands of the people.

Why, then, did the Reformation in Spain fail while it succeeded in some other countries? The most important reason was the Inquisition, which reached its full force in Spain and was more ruthless and cruel than any other instrument of persecution known in history. The second reason is that the movement lacked the support of the common people. Perhaps this was because most of them were illiterate and so conditioned to submission to clerical authority that they dared not oppose it. The majority of those who were reached by the Reform movement in Spain were of the professional and educated classes, and some were of the nobility.

The tragedy of Spain became the tragedy of Latin America. Under Renaissance concepts of political absolutism, the church and the state became unified as never before. The centuries-long struggle against Moslem invasion heightened the militancy of the Roman Church by making it an active partner in the political and military enterprise of driving them out of the country. The successful suppression of dissent and attempts at reform strengthened the power of the church in Spain. It was this authoritarian and dogmatic religion that the Spaniards brought to the New World.

HEIRS OF THE RENAISSANCE AND REFORMATION

Having outlined the distinctive characteristics of the Renaissance and the Reformation, as well as noted that there were some similarities, and having observed that the Spanish Reformation was snuffed out by violence, let us ask what these events have meant to the development of Latin America.

We are aware of the effect which later European movements and philosophic currents of thought had on Latin American culture; in another chapter we shall see how these philosophies influenced Latin America and produced a form of secularism and an active anticlericalism in the nineteenth century. We are dealing here only with the impact made by the Renaissance and the Reformation.

Broadly speaking, the United States has felt the influence of the Reformation while Latin America has felt that of the Renaissance. Anglo-Saxon America and Latin America are heirs of the same Western civilization; one fundamental reason why their history has been different is that the culture of the former came down through the mainstream of the Reformation, from the Hebrew-Christian tradition, while that of the latter came from the Greco-Roman world of the Renaissance. Waldo Frank says, "The men who settled North America, having broken with Rome . . . , were men not of the Renaissance, but of the Reformation." [9] He also says, "The conquistador, the padre, the *hacendado,* the clerk, who settled [Latin] America, were men of the Renaissance, men bursting with the immobile synthesis of Rome; yet still in love with it and bearing to America its gaunt body." [10] To quote a Latin writer: "The men who came to Mexico, first, to Peru and the Río de la Plata afterward, were undoubtedly legitimate representatives of the spirit of the Renaissance in all the lust of the flesh, the pride of the eyes, and the vainglory of life. In no respects were they the representatives of the Christian Spain of the Middle Ages and still less of the mystic Spain of Saint Teresa." [11]

One of the principal aspects of the Reformation was its emphasis on popular education, which is an essential element of democracy. This has been very much neglected in most Latin American countries. Although many Governments are making serious efforts to promote education, there is still a legacy from the past, and illiteracy figures continue to be too high.

The Reformation established the relationship between the widespread use of the Bible and democracy by placing in the hands of the ordinary man the source of revolutionary ideas regarding individual freedom and human rights. The leading Argentine writer, Sarmiento, once said, "It is the Bible which fertilizes the roots of democracy."

The question of individual liberties and rights as over against an external authority is of tremendous importance in any country, but particularly is it an issue in Latin America. Dean Inge says: "The one essential principle of the Catholic system is the control of the individual conscience by an authority or law placed without it, and exercised over it, by men assuming to act in the name of heaven." [12] The Reformation questioned, challenged, and broke away from the authority of the Roman Church and emphasized the dignity and rights of the individual, a cleavage that proved to be revolutionary in the social and political development of the northern countries of Europe and later of the United States.

An authoritarian, hierarchical religion conditions a people to the inequalities of the class system, to a stratified society with its injustices and handicaps, and to a lack of initiative and obligation in civic affairs. We find a ray of hope in the fact that, unprepared as they were for political independence and for democracy involving individual freedom and responsibilities, the Latin American people have shown repeatedly their desire for, and love of, freedom.

II

The Latin American
Scene Today

In the previous chapter we stated that the ideology that has exerted the greatest influence in shaping Latin American culture has been the Roman Catholic religion. If we are to have an adequate understanding of this vast and complex subject, we must also take into consideration the other factors we mentioned, as they too have had a significant part to play. It is our purpose, therefore, to deal in this chapter with some of these, namely, geography, economic, social, and political life, so that the reader may have a framework within which to view Latin America as a whole.

THE INFLUENCE OF GEOGRAPHIC FACTORS

The region we call Latin America is made up of twenty independent countries which may be grouped as follows: Mexico; Central America (Guatemala, Honduras, El Salvador, Nicaragua, Costa Rica, and Panama); the West Indies (Cuba, Haiti, and the Dominican Republic), and South America (Colombia, Venezuela, Brazil, Uruguay, Argentina, Chile, Paraguay, Bolivia, Peru, and Ecuador). Geographically the area also includes British, Dutch, French, and United States possessions, which politically and culturally are not Latin America. Exception should be made in the case of Puerto Rico; although it is a United States possession, it occupies a singular place because linguistically and historically it is in the stream of Latin American culture.

The Latin American countries cover an area of about eight million square miles, or two and a half times the size of Europe.

Brazil alone is larger than the United States and is surpassed among the nations of the world only by Russia, China, and Canada. The twenty republics vary in extension, topography, racial composition, natural wealth, and number of inhabitants; these differences account largely for the unequal stages of social, economic, and political evolution in which they are to be found. This diversity of conditions creates contrasting degrees of social and economic development even within a given country; therefore regionalism plays a very important part in every phase of the life of Latin America.

On the west coast of South America the vast range of the Andes (with Mt. Aconcagua in Chile, the second highest peak in the world) lifts its mighty ramparts to the clouds and runs unbroken from Panama to Tierra del Fuego at the tip of the continent. It confines Chile to a narrow coastal strip seldom more than a hundred miles wide and nearly three thousand miles long. It spreads out to form the wind-swept Altiplano of Bolivia and the lofty valleys of Peru, Ecuador, and Colombia. The Andean chain is part of a massive range which continues, at lesser altitudes, through Central America and up through North America. This Andean-Rocky system is the dominant physical feature in the American continent and has been a vital factor in determining rainfall, flow of population, and development. This highland-lowland apposition — the mountainous interior versus the lowland areas — explains sociological and political differences in Latin America; for example, those between Guayaquil on the hot coastal region of Ecuador, and Quito, the capital of the country, at an altitude of 9,300 feet. This also explains the divergence in outlook of the people of Barranquilla on the coast of Colombia and those who live in Bogotá, the capital city, 8,500 feet above sea level. Life in the sunny, balmy climate of the tropical islands of the West Indies is vastly removed from life in the lofty, barren highlands of Ecuador and Peru, or in the immense treeless pampas of Argentina.

Four huge river systems — the Magdalena, the Orinoco, the Amazon, and the Paraná — drain the subcontinent of South

America. The Amazon valley is the most extensive forest region in the world and the most sparsely populated. Jungle, rain, and heat have made it one of the great obstacles to the progress of man. José Eustacio Rivera describes the scene in the awesome forest: "At night unknown voices, phantasmagoric lights, funereal silences. It is death that passes, giving life. Fruits fall, and on falling, give promise of new seed. Leaves come to earth with a faint sighing, to become fertilizer for the roots of the parent tree. Crunching jaws are heard, devouring with fear of being devoured, warning whistles, dying wails, beasts belching. And when the dawn showers its tragic glory over the jungles, the clamor of survivors again begins." [1]

The plains of South America have played an important part in the history of several countries. Bolívar assembled his troops on the llanos of Venezuela in order to cross the Andes and defeat the Spaniards, liberating what are now five nations. Rosas was a Gaucho in the pampas of Argentina before becoming the ruthless dictator who ruled that country with fire and sword for twenty-three years. San Martín, the liberator of the south, started out from these same pampas and trained his men at the foot of the Andes, preparatory to crossing them and fighting a decisive battle which helped determine the fate of many of the South American republics.

The jungle, the desert, and the *pampa* are inhospitable and unfriendly to man; the mountain valleys and the coastal areas have largely been the focal point of life in Latin America for the civilizations that predated the conquistadores and for present-day populations. The great empires of the Aztecs in Mexico and the Incas in Peru developed in the plateaus and mountain regions; the Chimus and the Nazcas built their cities near the scant rivers of the arid Peruvian coast. It is true that the Mayas first established their amazing civilization in the lowlands of the Yucatán peninsula, but this is a heavily wooded area which cannot be compared to the dense jungles of the great river basins where the forces of nature are so forbidding.

Topography and climate have been important determining factors in the evolution of society. Throughout the course of Latin American history, towering mountain ranges, dense forests, and parched deserts have created natural barriers to intercommunication, and produced such differing conditions as to almost set populations apart as alien groups. Today, however, the picture is changing; a transformation is taking place in the life of the Latin American countries which is blurring somewhat the lines of demarcation set up by physical features and climatic factors. The expansion of air transportation and communication has resulted in penetration of even the remotest hinterlands. A network of airways circles and crisscrosses the area, reaching into the interior where it has been impossible to introduce the railroad or the automobile due to the inaccessibility of the terrain. Thus air traffic is taking over many of the services performed by surface transport in other countries. The possibilities for future expansion of air travel in the Latin American republics are practically limitless.

TWO LATIN AMERICAS — CONTRASTS

The tourist in Latin America who does not get off the beaten path and look beyond the façade presented by the glamorous modern cities will not be aware of the glaring contrasts between life in these metropolitan centers and that in other areas of these countries. He will visit cities such as Lima, Santiago, Buenos Aires, Rio de Janeiro, São Paulo, and Mexico City. (Latin America can rightfully boast of these; after New York and Chicago, the next four largest cities in the Western Hemisphere, from the point of view of population, are Buenos Aires, Mexico City, Rio de Janeiro, and São Paulo.) In these cities he will see Government offices, business premises, and apartments housed in towering skyscrapers; large department stores; factories springing up on the outskirts; huge stadiums and beautiful parks and tree-lined avenues. In some of the cities he will be impressed by immense university campuses with gleaming modern buildings. He will probably arrive at, and depart from, a great new airport with more spaciousness and conveniences than many an airport

in the United States. He will see numberless movie theaters showing the latest American, European, and Latin American films.
He will also be able to attend the legitimate theater and a variety
of lectures and other cultural activities such as concerts and art
exhibitions. He will stop at the most up-to-date hotels, where he
will find all the comforts and services of any first-class hotel in
Europe or the United States.

This is one Latin America; the other may well begin on the
fringe of the big city — and even the smaller town — and reach
out beyond it into the rural areas. It is the Latin America of the
majority of the people, the neglected masses, the poor, the semi-
literate or completely illiterate. Here are disease and misery; here
life is primitive and unorganized. Statistics reveal that in many
of the more backward areas people live at subsistence level; infant mortality is high and life expectancy can be as low as thirty
years. Taken as a whole, the people in these areas eke out an
existence under abject and deplorable conditions; their purchas-
ing power is extremely low, and their economic and political potential is stultified because they live on the margin of the national
life, receiving little and contributing little. It is the America of
the disinherited and the landless.

There is a growing consciousness among the more thoughtful
Latin Americans themselves that their countries will never make
any real progress while wealth is so unevenly divided and where
a few at the top enjoy the advantages of education, comfort,
leisure, and health, and the majority are almost totally deprived
of these benefits. More and more, Government officials, econo-
mists, writers, and other leaders in the Latin American world are
increasingly concerned about social and economic conditions,
and many are formulating programs for raising the standard of
living of the masses.

One outspoken writer is Luis Quintanilla, a distinguished Mexican diplomat and thinker, who wrote *A Latin American Speaks.*
One chapter in that book bears the title "Living and Dying:
Latin American Way." He says that of a population of 126 million (1943 figure) in Latin America, no fewer than 85 million

were starving and had no houses, beds, or shoes. He states that while it is popularly believed that the Latin American countries are rich, the truth is they are essentially poor. The myth of great wealth has been created by the exorbitant profits made by foreign investors. He refers to the inaccessible mountains, the impenetrable forests and endless deserts, and centuries of feudal exploitation. He says, "Vast rural domains, absentee landowner-ship, agrarian economy, lack of industries, disease, illiteracy, fanaticism, and a cleavage between wealthy minorities who do not work and millions of underdogs who do all the working: such are some of the evils characteristic of Latin America's backward economic pattern." [2] In 1951 the Minister of Economic Affairs in Ecuador stated that 95 per cent of the population of that country was undernourished.[3]

POPULATION GROWTH

The population of Latin America is the fastest growing in the world. The rate of growth is 2.4 per cent per year, which is twice that of the world as a whole. This phenomenal increase has taken place largely during the past thirty years, although the trend began at the turn of the century. In 1920 there were 91 million Latin Americans, and by 1953 there were 172 million, outstripping the population of the United States, which was estimated at 168 million in 1956. Population studies by the Bureau of Social Studies of the United Nations, published in 1955, indicate that should the present rate of increase continue, the population of Latin America will be 321 million in 1980.[4]

Apart from immigration, population growth depends on the differential between the birth rate and the death rate. In recent years Latin American Governments, with the co-operation of such organizations as the World Health Organization and the Technical Assistance Administration, have given greater attention to public health and to education leading to the dissemination of knowledge concerning sanitation and good health habits. Thus the death rate has been reduced, while the birth rate has been maintained. We get an idea of how far the Latin American

Governments must travel along this road when we realize, for example, that while the death rate in Chile decreased from 39.8 per 1,000 in 1930 to 15.7 per 1,000 in 1950, this latter figure was still 60 per cent higher than that of the United States.

Another fact that should be borne in mind when we consider the population of Latin America is its uneven geographic distribution. Almost half of South America is practically devoid of human habitation. Vast areas, such as the Amazon basin, Mato Grosso in Brazil, Patagonia in southern Argentina and Chile, and the Atacama desert in northern Chile, are very sparsely populated. While more than half of the people live in rural areas, there is a growing tendency to concentrate in urban centers, largely because of better employment opportunities. This trend is most pronounced in Uruguay, Argentina, and Chile. Brazil, more than any other country in Latin America, is in a position to encourage resettlement in its vast interior region. During the last few decades many cities and towns have sprung up in formerly undeveloped areas. Plans have been under way for several years to move the capital from Rio de Janeiro to Brasilia, a new city being built in the interior state of Goiaz.

The rapid rise of population in Latin America creates an ever-expanding demand for goods and services. For instance, the increase in Brazil's population by 13 million people in ten years (1940–1950) stimulated rapid industrial growth and expansion of markets. In 1949 Sears, Roebuck opened their first store in Rio de Janeiro. On the opening day, 123,000 customers poured into the store and spent the equivalent of $550,000. It is interesting to note that as a result of the new trend toward industrialization, 80 per cent of the goods sold were made in Brazil.[5] Since then Sears, Roebuck have opened stores in about thirty different places throughout Latin America.

ECONOMIC DEVELOPMENT

When we consider the economic development of the Latin American countries, we find rapid progress beginning in the early 1930's. In 1954, the total of goods and services was valued at

43.6 billion dollars, which was two and a third times the figure for 1945.[6] Latin America is potentially one of the earth's richest storehouses — once the obstacles to development and exploitation of its natural resources have been overcome — with a wide range of raw materials, foodstuffs, and minerals. It is predominantly an agricultural and mining region and, although a change is taking place in the total pattern, some of the countries are still one-crop or two-crop producers. It is easy to understand how this type of economy is more or less dependent on world market fluctuations in prices and demand.

Latin America occupies a key role in supplying raw materials to the United States, furnishing two thirds of the foodstuffs and a quarter of the industrial raw materials it imports. United States experts and industrialists argue that the Latin American countries can best foster their own economic development by increasing their basic materials for export. They point out also that industrialization must be accompanied by a growth in farm productivity in order to take care of an expanding population.[7] As a matter of fact, farm production rose about 50 per cent in the decade 1945–1955. The present trend, however, is toward industrialization. The Latin American countries seem to have one obsession in common, the desire to pull themselves up by their own bootstraps into the twentieth century, and they believe the way to do this is to industrialize. They hope to do in a few decades what it took the United States one hundred and fifty years to accomplish, availing themselves of improved technological methods and experience.[8]

Manufacturing production in Latin America, though still in its early stages, is 75 per cent higher than before World War II. Its total value is around ten billion dollars; this is between one fifth and one fourth of the total economic activity. The average manufacturing plant involves an investment of about $50,000, employs twenty workers, uses about two horsepower per worker, and produces one sixth as much as the average plant in the United States.

Food processing, textiles, steel, and cement are the main indus-

tries in Latin America. The first two, food processing and textiles, account for nearly 75 per cent of the manufacturing output,
the reason for this being that most of the countries produce the
raw materials for the two industries, relatively small capital investment is required, and the products can be sold on the local
market. The general increase in industrialization has occasioned
a shift in the pattern of food consumption. More people moved
to the cities, and as their standards of living rose, the demand for
processed food increased. In some cases food that used to be ex-
ported is now consumed locally.

The greatly increased production of cement is often taken as
an indication of the pace of Latin American industrialization. Before World War I, all cement was imported and consumption
was small. Most of the countries now have their own plants.

The production of steel is about two million tons a year, and
this supplies about half the local needs. This industry, of fairly
recent origin, faces formidable obstacles, such as lack of high-grade
coking coal (about 1 per cent of the world's reserves), high transportation costs, a small market, and a heavy investment of capital.

The Latin American industrial program needs outside capital
as well as production knowledge and management techniques
if it is to pass beyond the initial stage of development. Most
Latin American republics lack facilities for raising capital for
industrial development, since it is still true that private investment usually goes into real estate. Sound economic growth demands a balanced development, not only of industry but also of
agriculture, trade, mining, and power, with attention to health
and education.

The majority of people in Latin America still derive their
livelihood from the soil, but the number is slowly decreasing. In
1945 roughly 60 per cent of the people worked on the land,
whereas eight years later, in 1953, the percentage had fallen to
58.1. What accounted for this drop? Most of the people included
in this 1.9 per cent became industrial workers in the large cities,
while a few went into trade and construction projects. In many
instances they were not attracted by the prospect of higher wages

alone, but left rural areas because mechanized agriculture had displaced manual labor. This shift in population from rural to industrial occupation is causing concern. If Latin America is to maintain a rapidly growing population, it must greatly improve its agricultural production, which is a task of enormous proportions, involving bringing hitherto unused areas under cultivation — by irrigation of deserts, clearing of jungles, and so forth — and the introduction of scientific agricultural methods.

THE MEANING OF RAPID SOCIAL CHANGE

What do these tremendous changes mean to the Latin American people? A superficial impression might be that a rapid growth of population and a shift from an agricultural economy to an industrial one spell progress. In a sense they do, but it is also true that these changes greatly aggravate social, economic, and political problems. As has been pointed out, the conditions of poverty, disease, and ignorance, which prevail largely in the rural areas of Latin America, affect the lives of millions of people. Many of these people have drifted into the cities seeking employment, or have gone to mining centers and to work on road or other construction projects. In most cities the sudden influx of people has put a great strain on housing, food distribution, and transportation facilities; slums have arisen overnight; school buildings and equipment have become inadequate, and social services are overtaxed.

The new arrival in the city finds anything but the happiness and prosperity he expected. It is true that, if employed, he earns more, but the money goes almost as fast as it comes in. His needs are greater and more complex. With runaway inflation — which is the case in many countries — he finds his pay dwindling week by week. As Latin America lives within the orbit of the dollar economy, prices are correspondingly adjusted to compensate for the devaluation of the national currencies. Generally the margin of subsistence is so slender that in some cities a slight increase in bus or trolley fares has occasioned widespread strikes and rioting.

It can be said that in Latin America there exists a low-wage, high-income type of economy, which accentuates the separation between the "haves" and the "have-nots" and creates deep-seated bitterness among the masses as they see themselves failing to share in the augmented national wealth. It is a primitive capitalism superimposed upon a largely feudalistic structure, which has not yet felt to any extent the controlling force of organized labor or any other checks. Social legislation designed to protect the working class is not always applied in individual cases. Powerful corporations, both national and foreign, retain high-priced lawyers and are often able to avoid fulfilling their legal obligations.

Industrialization has become an ardently desired goal; businessmen seem to think that what makes the United States great and powerful are its gadgets, its automobiles, its refrigerators, its television sets — in a word, the things it produces — and they overlook its democratic traditions and the freedom its people enjoy, which are largely the fruits of its religious heritage and principles, and which are much more important than the material aspects of its civilization.

The growth of materialism as a philosophy of life is dangerous; it is based on the belief that life's problems can be solved on the material level rather than in the moral and spiritual realm. It overlooks the fact that the best-laid programs of economic or social development can fail utterly if the integrity of men is lacking and is unable to provide that underlying moral support without which plans for material improvement cannot be carried satisfactorily to fruition.

FERMENT, REVOLUTION, IDEOLOGICAL STRUGGLE

The idea of revolution has long been associated with Latin America, and it is true that some countries have had many different regimes in a matter of decades. Students of Latin American history, and more particularly the Latin Americans themselves, are familiar with the pattern of *caudillismo,* dictatorships, feudal oligarchies, militarism, clericalism, and imperialism in the

Latin American scene. The ferment of ideas and the sense of social injustice stir the people into a state of rebellion against an oppressive or corrupt dictatorship. This unrest produces further repressive measures to contain it. Sooner or later advantage is taken of the seething dissatisfaction — usually by a military man — and a *coup d'état* is staged, with a seizure of power. As no fundamental problems have been solved and the people's needs have gone unmet, the process soon starts all over again.

Three elements seem to be essential to a dictator, namely, the support of the Roman Catholic Church, the loyalty of the armed forces, and financial backing. Without all of these, his situation becomes precarious. For instance, the depression of 1929 in the United States had repercussions in Latin America, where some of the dictatorships, unable to maintain themselves in power under the straitened economic conditions, were overthrown.

In recent years, however, there has been a tendency toward more orderly and peaceful changes of government through elections. Industrialization has been a factor favoring this development, because it tends to strengthen an emergent middle class without which there cannot be real political stability and democracy.

During World War II, the Latin American countries lined up with the Allied nations. The four freedoms were enunciated by the United States and Great Britain as the objective of the struggle. However, many of the Latin Americans were painfully aware that these freedoms were denied to them. A typical reaction was that of a group of Peruvian students who read a poster printed in the United States. It depicted the four freedoms, and when the students saw it they said, " That's fine, we are all for them, but we don't have any of them in our country."

Then came the end of the war and the beginning of the cold war. In the anti-Communist struggle the United States, home of rebellion against oppression and leader of political independence and freedom, has appeared to the Latin Americans to assume the role of the political conservative and the reactionary. The Western powers, on the whole, seem anxious to prevent change if possible, though the times call for it and it is the trend of history; they are conservatives in a radical age. The Latin American dictators have been quick to sense this, and they have seized upon a new weapon with which to suppress the demand for justice and human rights and even to deny religious freedom for minorities. The way to defeat the liberals and the progressive elements is to call them Communists. " The anti-Communist flag in Latin America," said former President Eduardo Santos of Colombia, " is being converted into a pirate's flag. The worst enemies of liberty hoist the anti-Communist flag and hide behind it. The loyal friends of democracy are accused of communism the moment this aids the dictators. Unfortunately, this despicable trick finds a sad approval in the United States." [9]

It is amazing how dictators can get away with putting up a façade of democracy and high-sounding declarations of freedom. Perón was a master at this sinister type of hypocrisy. He told the people, " We are fighting the oppression of gold and rank because they both mean suffering and tears for the people." [10] Perhaps the Brazilian writer Manoel da Nóbrega is right when he says that " twentieth-century man will go down in history as a demagogue." [11]

A distinguished Colombian writer, Germán Arciniegas, former Minister of Education in his country, speaks of the " visible and invisible Americas." [12] The visible America is the face turned officially to the outside world; it is the America of presidents, ambassadors, and official delegates to conferences — an America which controls the press and other means of communication. It is the America which gives a great deal of lip service to the ideals of freedom and democracy, for there is nothing to lose and everything to gain by so doing. But if the people back home should demand that same freedom, they must be suppressed in the name of law and order; arms, tanks, and even airplanes — probably bought from the United States — may be used against them. Arciniegas cites an incident that took place at the beginning of Perón's dictatorship. A group of Argentine ladies from some of the best families gathered in the street one day and began to sing the national anthem, which opens with these lines:

> " Hark, mortals, the sacred cry,
> Liberty, liberty, liberty! "

This was a demonstration protecting the curtailment of civil liberties, and Arciniegas states that the women spent the night in jail.

Which is the invisible America of which Arciniegas speaks? He means the underprivileged, oppressed America, the masses who suffer injustice, whose rights are forever being trampled in the dust, and who are deprived of all but the barest essentials of life. This is the raw material of revolution.

An outstanding Argentine lawyer, César Barros Hurtado, published a book entitled *América — Penurias de Libertad* (America — Trials of Freedom). The author speaks very plainly about what he calls the pseudo democracy of Latin America. In this hour of international confusion, he says, the eyes of the world turn hopefully to America as the cradle and bulwark of liberty and democracy. This appears to him to be an erroneous idea, and he points out that in the greater part of it, namely, Latin America, there are semifeudal nations where one family or one man has governed for decades, suppressing all opposition. In some countries there is the crudest kind of absolutism, the man in power being venerated like a god. The voice of the opposition is silenced, while the press, the radio, and every other form of communication are controlled by the government. Books, newspapers, and magazines from abroad go through the strictest censorship. In order to inform himself personally about the realities of the situation in some of these countries, Barros Hurtado had to have secret interviews with people in basements or on the top of a mountain. He found hatred, violence, and suspicion between one country and another. Only in six out of the twenty republics did he find any degree of democracy.[13]

Amid the social revolution, the interplay of economic, social, and political forces, the ferment of ideas among students and intellectuals, and the advent of labor as a force to be reckoned with, a battle for men's minds is taking place. Ideologies of the right and the left, fascism and communism with their totalitarian systems, and a materialistic philosophy are at work vying for the allegiance of the people.

Unhappily Latin America has lacked the moral and spiritual foundations of Christianity in its culture. An eminent South American writer and lecturer, Julio Navarro Monzó, put it this way: "Not only the greatest problem but also the greatest tragedy of Latin America seems to have been its struggle of a century to found and build up a real democracy. But the greatest of all tragedies, in reality, although much less apparent, has been that, confronted with such a problem, the leaders of these peoples have never had a consciousness of its moral and religious aspect." [14]

Political or economic problems ultimately involve moral values. In other words, there is no such thing as political or economic life apart from men whose acts are subject to moral law. Thus in all phases of the life of a nation, man is the most important factor and, as elsewhere in the world, the chief problem in Latin America is man himself.

III

Racial, Cultural, and Political Patterns

In 1918, Carlos Octavio Bunge, a leading Argentine sociologist, wrote an essay entitled *Nuestra América,* in the introduction to which he says: " The political organization of a people is the product of its psychology. Its psychology is the result of ethnic factors, as well as physical and economic environment." [1]

In the previous chapter, reference was made to the influence which the physical environment has had on the development of Latin American civilization. Consideration will now be given to its racial composition and the character, or psychological traits, of the Latin American people and the bearing these have had on their political life and cultural patterns.

RACIAL COMPOSITION OF THE LATIN AMERICAN COUNTRIES

In Latin America the population, as far as racial factors are concerned, is a human kaleidoscope. All the races of man are represented: white, brown, black, and yellow people are to be found there; it is a continent without ethnic unity or homogeneity. Broadly speaking, the Latin American people of today are the product of three migrations, namely, from Asia, Europe, and Africa. This is a fact of tremendous importance as we endeavor to understand the ethnic and psychological factors which have helped to shape these people in the New World. Each of these three racial groups has made its own contribution to Latin American culture.

Most anthropologists agree that the first immigrants to America, the people we call Indians, came from Asia, in all probability via the Bering Strait. The first Europeans came in the fifteenth century; they were the Spanish and Portuguese. In the nineteenth and twentieth centuries waves of immigration brought other Europeans, such as Italians, Germans, and British, who settled particularly in Argentina, Uruguay, Chile, and southern Brazil. The migration from Africa was an enforced one; beginning with the sixteenth century, Negroes were brought in as slaves.

There are today nearly twenty million pure Indians scattered throughout the Western Hemisphere. Less than half a million are to be found in the United States and Canada; the rest form the majority of the population in Ecuador, Peru, Bolivia, and Guatemala, nearly half that in Mexico, and substantial minorities in several other countries. When the Spaniards arrived in Latin America toward the end of the fifteenth century, the Indian population was almost as large as it is today. They were the Aztecs of Mexico, the Mayas of Guatemala and Honduras, the Incas of Peru, Bolivia, and part of Ecuador, the Chibchas of Colombia, the Araucanians of Chile, the Caribs of the West Indies, and other smaller tribes or groups.

The Indians of South America fall into two broad categories: the jungle Indians in the forests of the Amazon basin, savage and semisavage people, who live largely by hunting and fishing; and the highland Indians, who till the soil in the valleys and on the steep slopes of the Andes mountains. The former type is diminishing in number, while the latter has survived in spite of successive conquests, cruel oppression, and primitive living conditions in the rugged mountains.

The highland Indians are almost entirely unassimilated, living apart from the body politic, away up on the mountainsides, practically inaccessible both from the physical and from the psychological standpoint. The majority still live in a form of serfdom fastened on them after the Spanish Conquest; they are impoverished, superstitious, and ignorant — a melancholy people. Governments in Latin America have from time to time made numerous plans and projects to uplift the Indian, but up to now little progress has been made. Among the most promising efforts is what is known as the Andean Indian Program, with the participation of the Governments of Peru, Ecuador, and Bolivia, and the co-operation of the United Nations and specialized agencies. The program is based on the idea of community development, involving resettlement of Indians on the land, improved agriculture, handicrafts, machine shops, health and recreation centers.

A group of Latin Americans known as " cultural fusionists," made up of poets, philosophers, writers, professors, and anthropologists, believe that America must develop an autochthonous culture in which all races will be fused into the national body politic. Until the Indians and other races in certain countries are incorporated into the life of the nation, they argue, democracy will be a legal fiction and merely a theory. Other groups, on the other hand, advocate keeping the races separate and continuing the old pattern of feudalism and the dominance of the white race.

The Indians have made a notable contribution to Latin American culture and some of them have been outstanding. Dr. Julio C. Tello, a full-blooded Indian of Peru, who died a few years ago, was one of these. He became one of the leading archaeologists in South America and was well known in the United States and Europe. Benito Juárez, another Indian, became one of Mexico's great presidents. General Cándido Mariano da Silva Rondón, almost a full-blooded Indian, has been the guiding spirit for many years of the enlightened Brazilian Indian Service.

The first group of whites to arrive were the Spaniards, who conquered and colonized in the fifteenth and sixteenth centuries. The descendants of the settlers who followed the first wave of conquest are among the leading families of some of the Latin American countries today. The next group of white people came as immigrants or settlers in the nineteenth and early twentieth centuries; they include Spaniards, Portuguese, Italians, Germans, British, Czechs, and Hungarians. The majority of these migrated to Argentina, Uruguay, and Chile, because the climate was more nearly like that of their native Europe. In addition, many Europeans have settled in boom cities such as São Paulo in Brazil and Caracas in Venezuela in recent years.

The Negro is to be found principally in areas with tropical climates, such as Panama, in Haiti and other countries in the West Indies, and in the coastal regions of Brazil, Peru, Venezuela, and Colombia.

The origin of the presence of the Negro people in Latin America goes back to early colonial times. The Spanish conquistadores had established themselves as overlords and exploiters and the Indian was enslaved as a laborer in the mines and in the tropical plantations, but as early as the beginning of the sixteenth century it was discovered that this enforced labor, together with the spread of European diseases, was rapidly exterminating him, and African slaves were brought in. The Portuguese had been engaged in the nefarious slave trade along the African coast since the middle of the fifteenth century. The British now joined in the lucrative business and it was estimated that, over a long period, about twenty million Negroes were brought as slaves to the New World, the larger proportion, however, to the United States.

The Asiatic race is represented by Chinese and Japanese immigrants who have settled in certain areas on the west coast of South America, in Central America, the West Indies, and Brazil. (During 1956, 9,000 Japanese immigrants arrived in Brazil.) The Japanese in the latter country number nearly half a million and they live mostly in settlements or colonies, although there is an increasing tendency for them to be assimilated in the general population. One can see young Japanese men and women in airline offices and business houses in São Paulo whose native language is not Japanese but Portuguese.

Besides being the most numerous element of the population the mestizo, a hybrid of the Spaniard and the Indian, is perhaps the most important, at least in thirteen of the Latin American countries. He is considered by some as the hope of Latin America. Dr. Samuel Guy Inman says: "The mestizo is the real Latin American. . . . [He] is a new spirit embodying the desires and sentiments of a new people, reared in the atmosphere of the New World." [2]

The mestizo is providing the bulk of the workers in the present period of transition and rapid social change. He is the skilled laborer, the mechanic and technician, the clerical worker, the businessman, and, to a certain extent, he is to be found in the medical, legal, and teaching professions and in politics.

The difference between the racial composition of the United States and that of Latin America is of great significance in the cultural, social, and economic development of these two divisions of the Western Hemisphere. In the United States the stock is largely European, with a Negro minority and a much smaller Indian one. The Indian was either displaced or eliminated. It is said that the early settlers " fell on their knees and then on the aborigines." In Latin America there is a preponderance of Indian, mestizo, and Negro elements, with a white minority. An important point to remember in comparing the United States and South America, as far as racial composition is concerned, is that the settlers in New England were fleeing from religious persecution and restrictions and that they came with their families to make new homes. Moreover, miscegenation was frowned upon in the United States. " Disapproval of racial crossing in the United States was not biological; if anything, it was religious and social." [3] On the other hand, the early Spaniards left their women-folk behind in Spain and came to Latin America in search of adventure or fortune. Miscegenation took place on a large scale and was a generally accepted practice among all classes. Thus in some Latin Americans' veins runs the blood of the Spaniard (or Portuguese), the Indian, and the Negro. Bunge says that this triple ancestral base has formed the psychology of the republics that came into being in the nineteenth century.

PASSION, INDIVIDUALISM, AND PERSONALISM OF THE SPANIARD

James Bryce said that all the Spanish American countries remain in a sense Spanish, having the broad features of Spanish character and temperament.

Spain lives on in the New World, in its culture, in its language, and in its soul. Not that Latin America is a mere replica of Spain, for the process of differentiation between the mother country and the daughter colonies began when the Spaniards first set foot in the New World and found themselves in a new and strange environment of large dimensions, richness, and variety. The descendant of the Spaniard has become the *criollo;* customs and manners have changed with the times, but the soul of the Spaniard continues to live on in the former colonies.

Therefore, in order to understand the Latin American character, it is essential to analyze the Spanish temperament, for, as we have seen, Spain has provided its dominant characteristics.

In 1928 the noted Spanish writer Salvador de Madariaga, expert on international affairs and former professor at Oxford University, wrote an original and interesting essay in the field of comparative psychology, under the title of *Englishmen, Frenchmen and Spaniards.* Originally given as a series of lectures, the work was written while the author was Director of the Disarmament Section of the League of Nations. He realized the importance of the psychological factor in politics, and maintained that the real solution of political problems depends on the human factor — men rather than material considerations are the soul of politics. Madariaga's essay is a study of the dominant characteristics of the three peoples mentioned in the title. He calls these a " characteristic impulse manifesting itself in a complex psychological entity, an idea-sentiment-force peculiar to each of the three peoples." [4] The three impulses, or systems, are: in the Englishman, fair play; in the Frenchman, *le droit;* and in the Spaniard, *el honor.* Interestingly enough, these three words cannot be translated with fidelity into the other two languages. The psychological center of the English people is action; of the French, intellect; and of the Spanish, the soul or passion.[5] The most important concern of the Spaniard is to " save his soul," and this phrase is not to be interpreted in the religious sense, but rather in the psychological, for it means to " maintain the spontaneity and integrality of the individual passion in the face of social activity, of generally accepted ideas, and above all, of collective passions." [6]

The predominance of passion over the intellect and the will can be seen in Spanish art, literature, and religion, for it is through passion that the Spaniard touches reality. Landscape plays an insignificant part in Spanish art; man is the center, man complete, precise, and individualized. The Spanish masters have filled the art galleries with unforgettable faces. The same concentration on man characterizes literary works such as those of the great Cervantes. In Spanish religious life, individual passion predominates, two outstanding examples being Ignatius of Loyola, the founder of the Society of Jesus and the leader of the Counter Reformation, and Santa Teresa de Jesús, the foremost Spanish mystic, so typically Spanish that she is unthinkable outside of Spain. In the life of Santa Teresa we find a pronounced characteristic of the Spanish soul — that it appropriates or annexes to itself the object of its worship. Some of her exquisite lines speak of making God her captive, so that her soul can be free. The religious approach of the Anglo-Saxon, or, shall we say, of Protestantism, is quite different, as can be seen in the lines of the hymn:

> " Make me a captive, Lord,
> And then I shall be free."

When Paul said he was " a prisoner of Jesus Christ " he meant it in a dual sense, physically and spiritually, because at the time he was imprisoned in Jerusalem.

We have seen that the Spaniard is a man of passion; he is also profoundly individualistic. " Unique, naked, primitive individuality has been the chief characteristic of the Iberian race," says Dr. John A. Mackay.[7] It is important to be clear as to the meaning of the word individuality or individualism, as it is the key to the Spanish character, and one of the main traits of the Spanish American. It does not necessarily mean egotism, or selfishness, but rather that the self provides the standard for determining the place of other social entities. Thus the self dominates the scale of values and relationships, and provides it with a subjective standard.

The man of passion, then, is an individualist who brings to collective life and action a subjective standard. He lives his life like a novel, and laws, regulations, and customs, i.e., the social framework of collective life, are not instruments for transmitting the pressure of the group, but entities that the individual may use for his own experience and action. In other words, he personalizes the law and nature itself. In the Spanish character there is a profound sense of justice, which Dr. Mackay calls "an abstract sense of justice."[8] Perhaps at no other time in the history of the Spanish people was this sense of justice so marked as during the conquest and settlement of the New World. This may sound strange in the light of the known facts regarding the cruelties perpetrated by the Spaniards against the Indians, yet an analysis of the historic records shows there were some forces at work trying to achieve justice in a legalistic and formal way.

In his noteworthy biography of Bartolomé de las Casas, Lewis Hanke, an outstanding North American authority on Spanish civilization, says: "It was inevitable that there should be a struggle for justice, given the nature of the Spaniards and the nature of the world. . . . Only the understanding of that struggle for justice will provide, in my opinion, the most revealing glimpse of the truth regarding the conquest of America."[9]

This same characteristic is also apparent in more modern times. An article in the magazine *Ibérica,* referring to events after World War II as far as Franco Spain goes, says: "Injustice, more than misery or sorrow, is what makes most Spaniards indignant. This strong sense of justice is an elementary characteristic of the Spanish people, and the injustice committed toward Spain in considering her unworthy of democracy, and in countenancing the regime which the Spanish people themselves have never accepted, is what brought their indignation to a culmination."[10]

Spanish individualism provides the basis of personalism which is so important in politics as in everyday life. Personal relationships transcend abstract principles and values in every sphere of activity, both private and public.

PASSIVITY OR FATALISM OF THE INDIAN

Some writers claim that the term "Latin America" is a misnomer, for it fails to recognize Indian and Negro contributions to that culture. An outstanding Brazilian novelist said, "I smile . . . when you call Latin Americans a people who have in their veins all kinds of non-Latin blood: Indian, Jewish, Dutch, Moorish, Negro, German." [11] The term "Indo-Afro-Ibero America" would be nearer the truth, but few would seriously advocate its use. The *Apristas*,[12] the political party of Peru favoring the development of the Indian, have used the term "Indo America," but that is just as unrealistic as "Latin America," since there are countries where there is a minimum of Indian blood. No satisfactory name that would express the different racial components has been found.

The dominant characteristic of the Indian is a kind of Oriental fatalism. Some historians believe that this trait of the Indian in Mexico and Peru was responsible, in part at least, for the ease with which Cortés was able to conquer the former and Pizarro the latter. For instance, when Cortés arrived among the Aztecs, the Emperor Montezuma was convinced that the day of reckoning had come. In 1489 a comet swept over the central valley in Mexico; to the Aztecs it appeared as the fiery, trailing body of a serpent in the skies. Montezuma regarded it as an evil portent of the fall of his empire, and in 1519, when the fair-skinned Spaniards arrived in Mexico, he felt the end had come. Cortés was the great god Quetzalcoatl who had returned from the dim and distant past fulfilling legendary prophecy.

Among the Indians of the Inca Empire, passivity, a form of fatalism, reached such a point that they even allowed the emperor to limit their choice in marriage; personal preferences were subordinated to the paternalistic state. The eminent Bolivian writer, Gustavo Adolfo Otero, points out that the individual initiative of the Indian under the tutelage of the Incas was largely submerged or limited. The hegemony or absolutism of the state and a pronounced patriarchal system meant that many decisions were made by the state for the individual. "The elimination of political thought in the Inca regime by means of a patriarchal, autarchic system," this writer maintains, "killed all ambition and inhibited individual initiative. . . . The Spaniards, in order to displace Indian culture, relied on two forces: their own will to power, and the Roman Catholic religion." [13]

At the time of the Spanish Conquest, says Otero, there was a clash of two cultures, the individualistic culture of the Spaniards and the collectivist pattern of life of the Indian.

It is interesting to note another characteristic peculiar to the Andean Indian: his tendency to withdrawal or isolationism. He not only sought physical refuge in high valleys and mountain fastnesses in his flight from conquest, but he erected a barrier between himself and the outer world by retiring into his inner-most being.

The Indian's instinct for withdrawal is paralleled by the trait to which reference has already been made, his deep, atavistic melancholy, which expresses itself so eloquently in the plaintive notes of the *quena,* with which he voices his pent-up despair and anguish at his fate.

Warmth and Emotionalism of the Negro

We have outlined some of the psychological features of the Spaniard and the Indian; the Negro is the third racial element we must consider. The Negro brings to the Latin American amalgam an unrestrained emotionalism and a warm and affectionate nature. He is a creature of impulse and disdains or ignores rules and discipline; his character is much more volatile and disorderly than that of the stolid Indian. He has shown qualities of leadership; the names of some Negroes stand out in the struggles for freedom in the subcontinent. It is not without significance that Haiti, where the population is practically all Negro, was the first Latin American country to win its political independence from a European power, i.e., from France in 1804.

The Negro has also made a great contribution to music, art, and literature. Much Brazilian music today contains the primitive rhythms he brought to the New World from his native African soil, where music, both ritualistic and traditional, played such an important part in his life. The pulsing African beats have been incorporated into modern forms which are considered indigenous to Brazil.

Perhaps nowhere else in the world has the Negro adapted himself so well to his new environment as in Brazil. Torn from his cultural roots in Africa and brought over as a slave, he was able to sing at his work, and with his laughter bring a lighter touch to life, amid unfavorable circumstances and depressing conditions.

The Negro in Brazil not only adapted himself, but also became largely assimilated. Miscegenation was widespread in Brazil for four centuries and still continues; this partly accounts for the lack of race prejudice. " While upper-class white Brazilians may look down their noses at lower-class black Brazilians on social, economic, and cultural grounds, there are relatively few of the former who do not have somewhere in their own ancestry some trace of what people in the United States call ' Negro blood.' " [14]

The Psychology of the Latin American

We are now in a position to try to evaluate the psychology, or the character, of the Latin American.

The complexity of a collective character, or the character of a people, due to the variety of influences that help to shape it, and the fact that it is a dynamic, fluctuating entity, rather than a static one, make this analysis or evaluation difficult. It is peculiarly so in the case of the Latin American because of the admixture of three races. We must bear in mind that generalizations cannot cover all types and sections of the population. For instance, a first-generation Argentine of Italian descent and a Haitian of pure Negro blood are both Latin Americans. In other words, the variety of types included in the term " Latin America " is very great.

We have already seen that, taking Latin America as a whole, the mestizo represents the most numerous racial type, and that the tendency is for the Spaniard, the Indian, and the Negro to become minorities. The different amalgamations or combinations of the Spaniard, Indian, and Negro have produced the national psychology of each country, with all the variations due to the preponderance of one group or another. Subsequent immigrations from many parts of the world have further accented this racial composite, though their contribution has been relatively minor. In addition, other factors must be taken into consideration, such as climate and physical environment.

Bunge maintains that the three fundamental characteristics of the Latin American are indolence, sadness, and arrogance, and of the three, indolence is the most pronounced. In one of his visits to the Argentine, Darwin asked a Gaucho why he spent most of the day taking a siesta and the evening playing or amusing himself. Why did he not work and employ his time better? To this the Gaucho replied, "*Es tan largo el día*" (The day is so long). Why do today what you can postpone until tomorrow or next week?

Today a visitor to a bustling city such as São Paulo, Buenos Aires, or Mexico City will probably be inclined to disbelieve the dictum that the Latin American is indolent and that *mañana* is his favorite word. It may well be that the pace of life in a growing industrial city or commercial center is changing the character as well as the habits of the Latin American.

This procrastinating tendency, in moderation, however, has its good side. By comparison, the North American is a slave to time and the events happening around him. He is a hustler, he wants things to happen, and he must be punctual. Time is money. The Latin American is a slave neither to time nor to the machine. He will be late for appointments and will be profuse in his apologies, conveying the impression, however, that you did not really expect him to be on time. If you had meant seriously to indicate a certain hour and no later, you would have added, "*Hora inglesa*" (English time), since the Englishman is noted for his punctuality.

The Latin American has another redeeming feature which it is hoped he will not lose in the quickened pace of an industrialized society. It is an emphasis on personal relationships. We have seen that personalism is a distinct quality of the Spaniard; we find it also in Latin America. In business, in politics, and in everyday life, people are more important than things, and it follows that, conducted on this personal and more leisurely basis, mundane affairs often fall into their proper place. The North American businessman who transacts his business in Latin America on the basis of high-pressure salesmanship methods is likely to find that they are not so effective among people who put friendships and personal relationships first. Work is an adjunct to life in Latin America, not its main purpose.

As a result of his humanism or personalism, his individualism and his feeling for the wholeness of life, all of which he inherited from Spain, the Latin American has a theoretical and an idealistic, rather than a practical approach to problems. At the turn of the century, Enrique Rodó, the foremost Uruguayan writer of his generation, wrote his immortal essay entitled *Ariel,* which has had a profound influence on the thinking of Latin America as a whole. In this essay Rodó appealed to his fellow Latin Americans to keep their eyes fixed on the higher life and on the things of the spirit, which are superior to the material and the utilitarian. "The civilization of a people acquires its character," he said, "not from the manifestations of its prosperity or its material greatness, but from the superior ways of thinking and feeling that are possible within it." By temperament the Latin is the idealist and the Anglo-Saxon the activist.

The influence of Rodó's essay still remains in the minds of many cultured Latin Americans. They remember that he depicted Latin America as Ariel and the United States as Caliban. The former, he maintained, embodied high cultural achievements and values, while the latter was utilitarian, practical, and devoid of culture in the real sense of the word. It is true that Rodó had words of praise for the efficiency and inventiveness — as well as the democratic institutions and love of liberty — of the people of the United States; but his main criticism was not lost on the Latin American people, and it hurt relations between North and South. In recent decades Latin Americans have discovered in the United States some of the culture which they felt did not exist there, while industrialization has brought to their countries some of the practicality and efficiency of the North, along with some of its disadvantages.

The individualism of the Latin American rebels against the standardization and mechanization of life; man as a cog in a huge machine is an idea which he rejects as subhuman. He objects to being regimented; it offends his dignity as a person. The writer remembers the sharp criticism of a well-known Latin American writer and lecturer because he was given a number in a large barbershop in New York!

Closely related to the central psychological entity in the Spaniard, namely, *el honor,* is his *dignidad,* and this we find quite pronounced in the Latin American. It accounts for the great offense to the Latin American caused by the series of United States interventions which took place in a number of countries before the enunciation of the Good Neighbor Policy by President Roosevelt in 1933. The State Department in Washington has come to realize through painful experience how important sovereign rights and national dignity are to the Latin American people, even more important than material benefits or economic aid.

A sense of dignity and individual worth, together with a marked class distinction between the landowning groups who have lived a leisurely existence and the *peones* who have done all the work, have produced in the Latin American a disdain for manual labor of all kinds. Coupled with a marked formality in customs and manners, this contempt for manual work produces an avoidance of any task that could be performed by a menial; thus it is that a man would shrink from being seen in the street carrying even a parcel, lest the assumption be made that he could not afford a servant to do this for him.

Formality is seen in almost everything that the Latin American does, whether it be a social visit, writing a letter, or delivering a speech. The North American visitor to Latin America is always impressed by the frequent handshaking, as well as by the *abrazo* among friends. He will undoubtedly return to the United States telling everyone how friendly the Latin American people are, and for some time he will find himself shaking hands through a newly acquired habit. The *abrazo* is a little more subtle, as only experience will tell him whom to embrace and when, and so he laughs that off as something which only the Latin Americans themselves know how to do. The writer recently had an interview with a Latin American diplomat in the latter's hotel suite in New York. At the close of the interview pleasantries were exchanged and hands were shaken. The diplomat accompanied the writer to the door and shook hands again. He insisted on seeing him to the elevator, where there was a final handshake. Insincere? No; friendly and courteous and — for the North American — an unforgettable experience as well as a rare one in our northern latitudes.

A Sense of Tragedy

Individualism, dignity, formality, and ceremony are all present in the traditional Spanish spectacle, the bullfight, still popular in countries such as Peru and Mexico. Another element which must not be overlooked in the Spanish and Spanish American character, and which expresses itself so dramatically in the bullfight, is a sense of tragedy. The graceful ritual of the *fiesta brava,* inexorably dooming the poor brute to torture and death, symbolizes a tragic sense of life itself. The supreme moment when the *coup de grace* is administered is to the Latin the expression, in physical terms, of his own deep awareness of the inevitability of death. By way of contrast, the United States has a sense of mission and achievement; the North American is bent on conquering the material world about him, on producing bigger and better things and on accumulating wealth. The one is a sense of the tragic undercurrents of life, the other a drive toward fulfillment.

The Brazilian Character

The Brazilian people are rather sensitive about being included in generalizations regarding Latin America which are obviously based on the development and characteristics of the eighteen Spanish-speaking countries. While there are many cultural and racial similarities between Portuguese- and Spanish-speaking Latin America, there are also a number of differences.

Brazil is the colossus of the South — an immense country still in the process of developing and expanding, especially in its vast interior. Compared with the Spanish-speaking countries, Brazil has had a much less turbulent political history, prior to and since the formation of the republic in 1889, which in itself was a peaceful event.

The Brazilian character is also the result of many factors, including the ethnic contribution of the three peoples — Iberian (Portuguese), Indian, and Negro — the cultural inheritances from Portugal and Africa, and the various geographic, economic, and social conditions.

Unlike the Indian of the Peruvian, Ecuadorian, and Bolivian highlands, the Negro of Brazil is today an active member of the body politic, having had some access to culture and been accorded a place in social life almost from the time he was first brought to the country. According to Gilberto Freyre, leading Brazilian sociologist, many of the Negroes who were shipped as slaves came from areas where Negro culture was most advanced, such as the north of Africa, particularly the Sudan.[15]

In the early days the Negro was an integral part of what was an important institution in the life of the colony, the sugar plantation system. The Portuguese settlers who owned these plantations have been called "vertical founders" because they struck their roots down deeply and built solidly their stately mansions (*casas grandes*). The Negro quarters were called *senzalas*. Life for these plantation dwellers was more or less self-contained; they had their own private chapels, churches, and schools. Freyre calls the more adventurous Portuguese settlers in early Brazil "horizontal founders"; they were nomadic, migratory frontiersmen known as *bandeirantes*, who lived outside the restraints of the religious and social life of the plantations or cities. They began the process of colonization of their country which continues to this day.

As in the case of the Spanish-speaking countries, Brazil has inherited from Iberia a pronounced individualism. It is often rebellious and aggressive, and is closely allied to the arrogance of the Iberian people. In Brazil we find also a distinct regionalism due to the juxtaposition of small and large states without much contact with one another; these two characteristics, individualism and regionalism, have produced a tendency toward non-co-operation, which has serious implications for political life.

From the amalgamation of three races and the peculiar social formation of the Brazilian people comes a marked predominance of sensibility over intellectualism. The Brazilian is known not so much for the vigor and profundity of his thought and reasoning, as for his brilliance, grace, and emotionalism. As one moves about among the people, whether it be in the large cities or in the interior, one feels that there is a graciousness, a kindness, and a sensitivity which are very pleasing and winsome. Freyre attributes this partly to the influence of the Negro element. " He gave us a revelation of a kindness greater than that of the whites," he says, " of a tenderness such as Christians do not know, of a warm, voluptuous mysticism with which he has enriched our sensibility, our imagination, and our religiosity." [16]

LATIN AMERICAN POLITICAL LIFE

The term *política criolla,* so well known south of the border, is difficult to translate into English, since it is something typically Latin American. We might call it " local politics," but that does not convey adequately the meaning of the term (in Spanish). It means the cleverness, adroitness, or facility for intrigue displayed by the *caudillos* or political chieftains as aspirants for power. Once in office, their objective is to stay in and rule, rather than to go down in history for their wisdom and statesmanship. Not only are the fortunes of the politician himself involved in all kinds of maneuvers and machinations, but also those of his family, relatives, and friends. That is why a revolution in Latin America usually means a complete turnover of government personnel with the consequent political instability resulting from a lack of continuity in administration.

We have noted the importance of individualism, as well as the influence of regionalism and the lack of co-operation or social consciousness in Latin American life; these traits are carried over into political life as well. The appeal to the voters is on the basis of personal prestige rather than platforms. Political parties often carry the names of their heads, usually presidential candidates, instead of names suggesting social or economic theory or doctrine of one kind or another. The public has very little concept of what lies back of political programs, and less understanding of their content and implications. A successful revolution is usually a dramatic event in which the leader catches the imagination of the populace and becomes the man of the moment. In an election the voter does not attach too much importance to his vote, for his individualism militates against his co-operating with fellow voters for social ends. Men rather than ideas dominate political life in most Latin American countries.

This emphasis on personalism in politics, plus the tendency of the people to carry over into political life their veneration of the Virgin and of the saints, has led to the deification of dictators. This process is accentuated by the group surrounding the dictator, who stand to gain most from his continuation in power. "God and Trujillo" are the signs to be seen in the Dominican Republic; "Perón, King, Lord," shouted the crowds in Argentina in 1950, while "Saint Perón" was on the lips of many. The extraordinary feature about the Perón regime was the unique personality of Eva, his wife. She — perhaps more than her husband — succeeded in setting herself up as a symbol of the feelings and aspirations of the masses. Her message to the Argentine people on Christmas Eve, 1950, is a good example of this identification. "I raise my voice," she said, "humble as it is, united in purpose with him who loves you as no one else loves you, because no one has given himself heart and soul to his people as he has: General Perón. My words are directed to the heart of every one of you, and on this night of hope I offer you my very life, if by so doing I can dry a single tear. . . . I leave with you my love and my faith in Argentina and in you. My joy tonight is your joy, as the sorrow you have suffered is also mine."

It is true that attempts have been made in some countries to inject social doctrine and ideas into politics, the outstanding examples being the Argentine Socialist Party, the Batllista Party in Uruguay, and the APRA [17] in Peru. It is doubtful, however, whether the Aprista movement would have assumed such importance and recognition had it not been for the dynamic, magnetic personality and crusading spirit of its founder, Víctor Raúl Haya de la Torre. Powerful forces from both the right and the extreme left have until now prevented this movement from changing radically the political life of Peru, but some impact has been made on the Latin American scene in the direction of social reform.

There is another feature of the Latin American character that comes from that of the Spaniard which we should like to mention in passing: his arrogance will not allow him to suffer another to succeed while he does not himself do so. Bunge tells the story of a fair in which an Englishman, a Frenchman, and a Spaniard were trying to climb greasy poles. As the Englishman began to climb, his friends smoked their pipes and watched him. As the Frenchman began to climb, his fellow countrymen urged him on and made frantic efforts to encourage him. The Spaniards pulled their contestant down by the legs.

THE IMPACT OF PHILOSOPHICAL THOUGHT ON POLITICS

While it is true that man rather than things, and men rather than ideologies in political life, assume importance in the Latin American countries, we must not overlook the fact that philosophical ideas have had great influence upon the thinking of those who have directed their destinies, particularly since independence from Europe was won.

Latin America has not produced many outstanding philosophers or thinkers, but leaders of thought have shown a facility in absorbing ideas from other countries. According to Professor Northrop of Yale University, the main factor in the development of thought and culture during the past hundred and twenty years has not been the issue between Spaniards and Portuguese on the one hand and Indians and Africans on the other, but rather that modern philosophical, political, economic, anticlerical, and even antireligious ideas have been in conflict with Roman Catholic medievalism emanating from Europe.

It is true that the Anglo-Saxon world, and in particular the United States, has been exposed to the same philosophical and ideological movements, but with this important difference: that while North America was Protestant, Latin America was Roman Catholic. Anglo-Saxon North America, as we have seen, was influenced by the Reformation, whereas Latin America was influenced by the Renaissance. North American culture felt the impact of the Reformation before coming into contact with modern philosophy and new theories on education, economics, and politics, and was able to reject Aristotelian and medieval ideas in secular institutions while still retaining basic religious principles and values. In Latin America, as in France — neither of which was influenced to any extent by the Protestant Reformation — the rationalism, Comtian Positivism, and Encyclopedism of Europe have produced a strong current of anticlericalism and even atheism.[18]

Comtian Positivism has had a particularly strong influence on the cultural life of Brazil during the last half of the nineteenth century, and still continues to do so.[19] The emphasis on humanity and its nonsectarianism appealed to Brazilian idealists. The first Positivist Society in Brazil was founded in 1870, and in 1897 a temple was erected in Rio de Janeiro with this inscription: "Love the principle, order the basis, progress the end." When Benjamin Constant, a leading Positivist, became influential in the founding of the Brazilian republic, the words "Order and Progress" were placed across the Brazilian flag, the word "Love" being omitted.

A reaction against Positivist philosophy set in at the end of the nineteenth century; the new movement called Humanism took in every dimension of human culture, experience, and civilization around the world. The Mexican Revolution of 1910 was a practical expression of this movement, and it is not without significance that the educational building erected about that time in Mexico City contains four figures: Quetzalcoatl, representing the Indian; de las Casas, the synthesis between Roman Catholic

Christian values and Indian life; Plato, classical Western culture; and Buddha, the religious and human values of Asia. It is not surprising that the Mexican Revolution still means a wide variety of things to different people. It can be said that it is the most serious attempt until now to redeem the Indian and educate the masses of Mexico, overcoming the influence of the Spanish Conquest and reviving old values that had been lost.

Another unique experiment of a totally different kind is that of Uruguay in South America. This country did not face the problem of combining the values of the Indian and those of the European; its situation was comparable to that of the United States in that the Indians were very early pushed back or exterminated. Uruguay, like Mexico, felt the influence of the Positivist and Humanist movements. While French Encyclopedist ideas influenced the early leaders of the country, the constitution of the Commonwealth of Massachusetts was chosen as the model for that of Uruguay, instead of the Constitution of the United States, because Uruguay preferred not to be strongly federated. Batlle y Ordóñez, the great statesman who came to power early in this century, was opposed to the system of a presidency and in favor of an executive council. In 1951 this became a reality, and thus Uruguay is the only country in Latin America which has a council instead of a president.

However, it is an open question whether Latin America's political troubles can be cured by such expedients as substituting a council for a president. Democracy is a political system in which sovereign power is vested in the people, not only in theory, but actually. Most Latin American countries have only recently emerged — some of them have not yet done so — from the colonial type of society. There is a small rich class, which holds most of the social and political power in its hands, and a large uneducated and impoverished class. In between is a developing middle class, growing, as we have seen, in some countries, due to industrialization. The Roman Catholic Church, which has dominated the Latin American countries for four centuries, is a totalitarian institution, and it has conditioned the individual to authoritarianism rather than to democracy.

It is interesting to note that while at the time the Spanish colonies in the New World won their independence from the mother country the existing social and political structure was far from democratic, yet the leaders of the independence movement and founders of the republics looked to the United States for a pattern of political constitution. Thus it can be said that a basic contradiction exists in their political and civic life; on the one hand, although the Latin American constitutions incorporate the principles of freedom and the rights of man, they are very often honored more in the breach than in the observance even by the very leaders who have sworn to uphold them. Respect for these values has not been woven into the warp and woof of Latin American life, and only a fundamental spiritual and moral rebirth will create a new society in which justice, truth, and freedom prevail.

PROTESTANT BASIS OF POLITICAL INSTITUTIONS

A few years ago there appeared in Colombia a book entitled *La Estirpe Calvinista de Nuestras Instituciones* (The Calvinistic Origin of Our Institutions). The author, Alfonso López Michelsen, son of former President López, originally gave the content of this book in a series of lectures when he was a professor of constitutional law at the National University of Colombia. Professor López' thesis is simple, and yet its implications are of great significance: it is that the Latin American constitutions include the Calvinistic principle of the sovereign will of the people, and of government by consent of the governed.

On February 27, 1811, the first Constituent Assembly met in Colombia, and after thirty-four days of deliberations produced a constitution. This was a period of great upheaval in Europe and the beginning of the independence movement in Latin America. The constitution referred to the "sovereign will of the people." As López points out, up to that time the basis of authority, both in Spain and in the colonies in America, had been the pope and the Roman Catholic Church. Now, "by the irony of destiny," says López, "this most Catholic of Constituent Assemblies of

Colombia introduced the Calvinistic concept in our society." [20] In other words, the first constitution in the Latin American countries founded the authority of the state in the will of the people. All the constitutions of Latin America contain this principle, phrased in one way or another, and enshrined in the opening words of the Constitution of the United States: " We, the people . . ." It is interesting to note that in the Cortes of Cadiz, Spain, in 1812, in which the colonies were represented, a violent discussion took place over the phrase in the proposed Spanish constitution which said, " The Spanish union cannot be the patrimony of a person nor of a family — that sovereignty resides essentially in the nation."

Political authority in Spain and in the Spanish American colonies had its origin in the divine right of kings to govern. Calvin was the forerunner of the democratic state in that he maintained that authority is vested in the people, and he erected a democratic church system which came to be known as the Presbyterian system. In his famous *Institutes,* Calvin gave juridical structure to the concept of a church with no authorities save those chosen or elected by the faithful, i.e., the members. From this concept came the basis for representative government in a democratic state. It was John Locke, the Puritan philosopher, who gave this concept political form, particularly in his *Treatise on Government.*

López goes farther and maintains that the Calvinistic organization of society creates the political party system, since Calvin upheld the principle of free examination, both in religious and political matters — a principle not admitted in the Roman Catholic world. In a later book López states that the right to be wrong is a principle inadmissible both in the Roman Catholic Church and in the totalitarian state.

Thus we have the rather strange circumstance — as has been already noted — of countries, unprepared for democratic government because of their tutelage under an authoritarian church system, writing into their constitutions a fundamental principle of authority residing in the will of the people, which is the *sine qua non* of democracy. In other words, the democratic ideal is there, but as López — himself a Roman Catholic — says, the Latin American countries lack the Protestant background to be able to live up to the ideal.

Since many of the liberal, anticlerical leaders of Latin America have been rather negative on the contribution of Christianity to the democratic life of the republics, López' thesis is refreshing, and the words of Montalvo in Ecuador in the middle of the last century are also significant: " A sane and pure democracy has need of Jesus Christ." Montalvo believed that democracy would be the law of the nations " if someday the spirit of the gospel were to prevail." [21]

IV

Pre-Columbian Religions

It is not our purpose to describe in detail the civilizations or cultures that existed before Columbus reached America in 1492. Our main interest is in outlining the nature of the religions of the Indian, his beliefs and practices. A brief reference to the three main civilizations — the Maya, the Aztec, and the Inca — will help to give the proper setting for this study.

The more we come to know and understand these cultures, the more astonished we are at their achievements and the more we can appreciate the contribution the Indian has made to American life in this continent. The Spanish conquistadores must have been amazed to find such magnificent temples, causeways, and palaces, the latter filled with gold and silver and jade. The canals of Tenochtitlán in Mexico surpassed those of Venice, and the imperial highways of the Incas in Peru, piercing the snow-capped Andes for three thousand miles, spanning deep chasms and crossing lonely deserts, dwarfed the highways to be found anywhere in Europe.

Today visitors to the south of Peru and northern Bolivia are filled with wonder as they look upon the remains of the great stone fortress of Sacsahuaman above Cuzco, Machu Picchu — the Lost City of the Incas, or the ruins of Tiahuanaco. In all of these there is evidence of astonishing architectural and engineering skills. Huge granite stones, weighing twenty tons or more, were cut with such precision and fitted together so well that the ravages of time and the destructive force of earthquakes could not dislodge them; even today a piece of paper cannot be inserted between one stone and another. The Incas used the inclined plane, the crowbar, and the pulley, but did not have any other machines or even mortar for constructing their great buildings.

Surgeons performed delicate brain operations among the Peruvian Indians at a time when medicine and surgery were in their infancy in Europe. Long before the time of Pope Gregory, the Mayas evolved a more accurate calendar than the Gregorian, and were able to predict eclipses and chart the course of Venus with great precision. The Mayas developed a system of hieroglyphics, the first system of writing in the Americas. The Hieroglyphic Stairway at Copán in Honduras has the longest known Maya inscription, with 2,500 glyphs.

When we use potatoes, corn, beans, chocolate, peanuts, quinine, and tobacco, we should remember that we owe these and many other products to the Indian of the Americas. The discovery of corn was of great importance in the development of the pre-Columbian civilizations. No one knows how it was discovered; historians believe that when the early American men changed from a nomadic to a sedentary type of life, corn was probably the determining factor. Perhaps more than anything else the cultivation and use of corn helped to lift them from savagery to a relatively high degree of civilization.

It is no wonder that in the Maya, Aztec, and Inca civilizations, corn became such an integral part of the Indian way of life that it figures in their art, religion, and social customs in the form of corn dances, corn songs, corn goddesses, and corn rites.

THE MAYAS

The Mayas have been called " the Greeks of the New World," since they were a highly intelligent and artistic people who developed architecture, painting, mathematics, and astronomy to a surprising degree. The descendants of the Mayas, grouped in about twenty tribes, are to be found today in Yucatán, Tabasco, and Chiapas in Mexico; in Honduras and British Honduras; in Guatemala; and in parts of Salvador.

The beginnings of Maya history probably go back to around 600 B.C., but it is generally believed among archaeologists that there were two main periods of development, the Old Empire from A.D. 400 to A.D. 1000, and the New Empire from A.D. 1000 to A.D. 1400, although during the last two hundred years there was a fusion with Toltec culture. The word "empire" is not used here in the usual sense of the word, for in reality there was no empire and no emperor, but there were rulers of city states.

As in the case of ancient Greece, the Maya Empire was a cultural unit in which city states were bound together, a loosely associated group of powerful communities. The Old Empire reached its highest peak between the fifth and eighth centuries A.D., with cities such as Tikal, Uaxactún, Copán, and Palenque. For reasons which can only be conjectured, these and other centers of teeming population were abandoned, and the jungle took over. The new culture flowered in northern Yucatán, especially in the eleventh century A.D., in cities such as Mayapán and Uxmal. The greatest of them all was Chichén Itzá, the remarkable ruins of which came to light only in relatively recent times, after having been abandoned to the forest in the fifteenth century.

Religion was an integral part of the lives of the Maya people; their emotional and artistic temperament seemed to revolve around it. It was also the bond that united the tribes in a large federation of communities. Rituals began with birth and continued through the cycle of life. Astrology affected the child from the time he was born; during the first hours of his life a ritual was performed consisting of the flattening of the front part of the skull, since a sloping forehead was considered more beautiful than a straight one. Other ceremonies and rituals took place at puberty, during preparation for marriage, and the most elaborate of them at death.

The Mayas had many gods, to whom they prayed often and offered sacrifices of jade, fine feathers, and *tortillas*. When times of disaster or crisis came, they offered human sacrifices, though this practice was not as common as it was among the Aztecs. A visit to the Sacred Well at Chichén Itzá in Yucatán is an unforgettable experience, as well as a haunting one. There can be seen the platform from which maidens, chosen for their beauty, used to be flung into the forbidding, gloomy depths and somber waters of a well about two hundred feet in diameter, while thousands watched the ceremony. These sacrifices were made to appease Chac-Mool, the Rain God, the deity on whom crops and, therefore, human lives were believed to depend.

Chichén Itzá was the most important holy city of the Mayas, and Kukulcan was its patron deity. Another name for him was Quetzalcoatl, the god of the Toltecs and Aztecs. He was the god of the Sky and Thunder and, so legend said, it was he who appeared in human form to teach the people the arts of civilization. A ruler and teacher of this name did actually live among the Maya people and, according to one authority, died in A.D. 1208.

The symbolic representation of Kukulcan was the feathered serpent, which can be seen in many of the monuments and buildings still standing at Chichén Itzá. The feathered serpent is the symbol of light, life, and motion. The word *quetzal* is a Maya one used today for the bird of beautiful plumage to be found in Guatemala; *coatl* means serpent. Therefore, *quetzalcoatl* is the bird-serpent. His snake and water aspect brings him into relationship with the Rain God, and in his bird manifestation he is the Lord of the Sky.

Among the many gods revered by the Mayas, two stand out above the others — Kukulcan and Itzamná. The Mayas told the Spaniards that their ancestors had not worshiped idols until the coming of Quetzalcoatl, and that it was only after the Toltecs took Chichén Itzá that the plumed-serpent motif began to appear in the decorations of temples and other buildings. Itzamná was thought of as the god of gods, the creator of life, good and kind. However, because he was so aloof and remote from everyday life, he does not seem to have had much influence over it, and it was necessary to have many other gods and goddesses, one for almost every need and emergency. There were gods of corn, of agriculture, of travel, of war, and of death. The God of Death was pictured as having a grinning, fleshless skull and a body with protruding ribs. There were also goddesses of fertility, of weaving, and of suicide.

As among the North American Indians, nearly all the Maya deities had their opposite numbers, so that within the Maya polytheism there was a religious dualism. For example, while Itzamná was the creator god, there was a goddess of floods whose function it was to destroy; the beneficent Kukulcan had as his counterpart a god with a fleshless jaw who brought droughts. The Corn God seems to have been one who had no evil opposite; he was not challenged by the evil spirits, because he enjoyed the protection of the good ones.

The role of the Maya priest was very important. The chief priest enjoyed an authority equal to that of the head of the tribe. This dual chieftainship was not uncommon among other Indian tribes, notably in North America. The priests were the intellectuals or thinkers among the Mayas; two of the outstanding achievements of the jungle civilization must, therefore, be attributed to them — the invention of the system of hieroglyphics and their astronomical calculations, including the remarkable calendar dating back to 3000 B.C.

The flourishing Maya civilization had its golden age but, like any other, it was followed by a period of descent from splendor and magnificence. The outstanding figure in the later years was Kukulcan. According to legend, he did not die, but disappeared after prophesying that blond, pale-faced men would one day appear to conquer his people and that subsequently he himself would return as a sort of messiah to restore the Maya way of life. This is the legend that we have referred to as having impressed Montezuma, the Aztec emperor, and whose fulfillment he thought had come with the arrival of the Spaniards.

The Mayas today are a friendly, peaceful people, and they spend a good deal of time raising corn, as did their ancestors. The limestone in Yucatán is still of importance, but not so much as it was centuries ago when the Mayas were builders of cities and great monuments. They can no longer boast of a great civilization, but they can be proud of the achievements of the past.

"Today silent are the temples, courts, and colonnades; gone the rulers, priests, and sacrificial victims; gone the artisans and builders; gone these humbler folk whose unremitting toil alone made all this pomp and pageantry possible — back to Mother Earth, enshrouded by the living green of tree and bush and flower." [1]

THE TOLTECS AND THE AZTECS

Two cultures in the central valley of Mexico were outstanding, the Toltecs and the Aztecs. Thanks to some of the early Spanish chroniclers, following the conquest of the Aztecs, much more is known about the latter than about the Toltecs. Of the two, the Toltec culture was the superior, but most of what we know about them has come to us through the Aztecs and the Mayas, or is written large in the monuments they left behind, for they were the greatest builders in Central Mexico. Toltecs and Aztecs were of the same ethnological group, both speaking the same Nahua language. The Toltecs preceded the Aztecs, coming down from the north and settling in the central valley about A.D. 600. The Toltec monuments, consisting of huge pyramids surpassing those of Egypt in some respects, are to be found mainly in two centers, in Teotihuacán and Cholula. The Pyramid of the Sun at Teotihuacán has been restored, and thousands of tourists from the United States visit it every year; the ruins at Cholula are covered with rubble and vegetation. The Pyramid of the Sun is about two hundred feet high; although the temple is no longer there, it stood at one time at the summit, in a commanding position, overlooking all the other buildings. This was the temple to Quetzalcoatl, the same god that was taken southward by bands of migrating Toltecs and, as we have already pointed out, was later worshiped by the Mayas.

Teotihuacán, covering an area of about nine square miles, was not a civic center, but a great religious one; the most imposing buildings were temples, and the houses surrounding them were for those engaged in religious activities. The writer got the same impression from a visit to Teotihuacán as he did from seeing the pyramids near Cairo. The massiveness and durability are striking, but where are the evidences of the everyday life of the thousands who helped build them? The question, naturally, is a rhetorical one. Teotihuacán is a symbol of the way in which the religion of a people can become so massive and burdensome that it dwarfs into insignificance the very individual it is supposed to help.

Coming from the north, the Aztecs arrived in the central valley of Mexico about A.D. 1325 and settled on the shores of Lake Texcoco; when the Spaniards came to conquer in 1519 the Aztecs were at the height of their power. According to legend it was their chief god, Huitzilopochtli, who guided them to the spot where they finally settled after many wanderings. The god appeared in a dream to one of his priests and told him that the people would find a great rock in the middle of a lake, with an immense *tunal* where an eagle had made its home. Another version has it that they would find an eagle perched on a cactus with a serpent in its mouth. The legend in this latter form is symbolized in the eagle, serpent, and cactus on the Mexican flag and on the coat of arms, and the city which the Aztecs founded in 1325, called Tenochtitlán, later became Mexico City, the great capital of the nation today.

Aztec culture seems to have been influenced by that of the Mayas; for instance, they had an advanced calendar and a form of writing by means of pictures, or pictographs. Tenochtitlán became a large, beautiful city with imposing government buildings and houses of cut stone for the rich and of adobe for the middle class, while the farmers and peasants lived in huts with thatched roofs such as can be seen today in rural areas in Mexico. Skillful engineers constructed great causeways leading to other cities near the surrounding lakes and erected buildings on piles. In the fifteenth century they built a ten-mile dike to prevent the lakes from flooding the city. Artisans worked with gold, silver, leather and stone, and also produced beautiful shell mosaics and pottery. Aztec farmers raised maize, prepared a beverage called *chocolatl* and an intoxicating drink called "pulque" from the maguey plant. Productive land was owned communally, some plots being reserved for the priests and the chief.

Religion dominated Aztec life even more than it did among the Mayas, and much time was spent placating the numerous deities. The people believed that if they failed to honor their gods with sufficient sacrifices and offerings, this neglect would have disastrous results and would bring on the end of the world. Each day, night, week, month, and year had its own god or goddess. Vaillant, outstanding authority on Mexican culture, divides this pantheon into the following categories: great gods, creative deities, fertility gods, gods of rain and moisture, fire gods, pulque gods, planetary and stellar gods, death gods, variants of great gods, and other gods. The latter include a monster god, twin of Quetzalcoatl, a god of health, spirits of women who died in childbirth, and a god who was a mischief-maker or backbiter.[2]

The Aztec year was divided into eighteen months of twenty days each, plus a five-day period which was considered unlucky. An elaborate array of ceremonies and rituals filled the year, so that the people were not prone to forget their religious duties. Shamanism,[3] sorcery, and witchcraft were common too. Offerings of food and clothing were presented to the gods, but the chief offering was blood, or the human heart. It is well to try to understand just what was involved in the human sacrifice that was so common among the Aztecs. Religion had little to do with the perfection of the individual, but it was greatly concerned with the survival of the community. The rhythm of the universe, as they understood it, was closely bound up with the vast array of gods who controlled the powers of nature; for man to survive, the gods must be kept strong, for they permitted the very existence of man. It was believed that human blood offerings were vital to the well-being of the gods.

The idea of sacrifice is common to many religions throughout all ages. Parting with precious possessions is somehow related in the mind of primitive man with the acceptability of sacrifice. The more treasured the possession, the more efficacious it was thought the sacrifice would be; to the Aztecs the most precious gift was life itself.

The vast majority of the victims were prisoners, which was a rather convenient arrangement. Thousands of men, women, and children were sacrificed each year. One special type of victim stood out, for he was chosen to impersonate the god Tezcatlipoca himself, a god borrowed from the Toltecs, also called Smoking Mirror. The most handsome and intelligent young man was chosen from among the captives, and for a year before the sacrifice he was treated like a king and was instructed by the priests. As he wandered about from place to place, he was feted and even worshiped like a god, for he was considered to be the image of the god. A month before the final event, he was given four lovely maidens who had been specially reared. The victim was an impressive figure as he wandered about, playing his flute, with a garland of flowers on his head, wearing a necklace of precious stones and ornaments of gold on his ears, arms, and feet. On the appointed day he bade farewell to his wives and led the great procession up the steps of the pyramid to the sacrificial temple on the summit, breaking a clay flute on each step. At the top he was seized by black-robed priests and held down while a red-robed priest plunged a knife into his breast, tearing out the warm, bleeding heart and offering it to the god Tezcatlipoca. It was believed that the youth's soul would ascend into the highest Aztec heaven.

Some victims died in sacrificial combat, a ceremony described by a Franciscan monk named Bernardino de Sahagún who lived among the Aztecs about A.D. 1530. The scene took place in an enclosure large enough to hold thousands of spectators. In the center was a large circular stone platform, with a hole in the middle through which passed a rope tethering the victim. After an elaborate ceremony with processions and music played by priests on trumpets and flutes, the unequal combat began. Four warriors, two of them named " jaguars " and two " eagles," armed with swords and protected by shields, attacked the captive, who had no shield and only a sword edged with feathers. One by one the four engaged him, and it was not infrequent for the victim to wear out all four combatants, in which case a fifth was added. When the captive was overcome, he was sacrificed in the manner already described. Occasionally he outfought all five and was set free.

To our modern conscience the idea of human sacrifice in religious rites is abhorrent, and we shudder at the thought of its being practiced at all, let alone on such a scale as it was among the Aztecs; yet for them it was a ceremony that was basic to their view of the universe. If captives were not taken and sacrificed to the gods, then these would weaken and be unable to make the earth fertile and cause the sun, moon, and stars to move across the sky. It is not so long ago that the iniquity of Negro slavery and the slave trade did not affront the conscience of some Christian people; today there are many who still condone war with all its horrors and destructiveness. An Aztec's justification of human sacrifices might find a parallel in a Christian's rationalization of slavery and modern war.

Despite these cruel aspects of the religion of the Aztecs, the people themselves were mostly kind and gentle; they had a love for flowers, music, dancing, and dramatic performances. They excelled in literature too, and the following lines are an example: "Banish care; if there are bounds to pleasure, the saddest life must also have an end. Then weave the chaplet of flowers, and sing thy songs in praise of the all-powerful god; for the glory of this world soon fadeth away. Rejoice in the green freshness of thy spring; for the day will come when thou shalt sigh for these joys in vain; when the scepter shall pass from thy hands, thy servants shall wander desolate in thy courts, thy sons and the sons of thy nobles shall drink the dregs of distress, and all the pomp of thy victories and triumphs shall live only in their recollection. Yet the remembrance of the just shall not pass away from the nations, and the goods of the things of this life are but lent to us, its substance is but an illusory shadow, and the things of today shall change on the coming of the morrow."

The Aztec concept of the universe had a direct bearing on religion. We view the universe in a geographic framework or setting; the Aztecs saw it in a religious one. There were two worlds, the horizontal and the vertical. The horizontal world consisted of the center, occupied by the Fire God and the four cardinal points. The Rain God and the Cloud God dwelt in the East. The Lord of the Dead was associated with the North, a gloomy place. The South was presided over by gods related to spring and the flowers. The West was the home of Venus the planet, often associated with Quetzalcoatl, represented as the God of Knowledge.

The vertical world went in two directions, up and down, but the Aztecs' heavens and hells seem to have had no moral significance. There were thirteen heavens, the dwelling places of the gods according to their rank in the hierarchy. Those who went to heaven were assigned to a particular one; for instance, a warrior dying in battle went immediately into the presence of the Sun God as he journeyed across the sky, while one who died by drowning went to the heaven where Tlaloc, the God of Rain, presided. Similarly, in the underworld there were nine different regions, and, according to some authorities, it was believed that the dead spent four years in each of them before arriving at Mictlan, the Aztec equivalent of the Greek Hades.

As a result of this multiplicity of gods and ceremonies, the priests occupied an important place in Aztec life. As Aztec culture developed, the priest probably performed many civic obligations as well as religious duties. One body of priests was in charge of the worship and all the elaborate ceremonies and rituals connected with it. They were assisted by priestesses and many who aspired to be priests. Another group of priests devoted themselves to the education of the people in all that religion meant and implied, including the complicated astronomical computations related to the calendar and its bearing on religious observances.

When the Spaniards reached the shores of the New World and were able to observe the religions of the Indians, they were surprised to see some similarities between the pagan religion of the Aztecs and their own Christian beliefs. For instance, the Aztecs believed in the immortality of the soul, and there were even legends concerning resurrection after death. The cross was found in many places, and it appears in Aztec writings, although its significance was different from that of the Christian cross. They practiced a form of baptism, and the Spaniards were impressed by the fact that a child received a name during the ceremony and that water was used. There was also confession to Aztec priests and penance for sins, as well as fasting and the observance of holy days. A form of communion somewhat similar to that of the Roman Catholic Church was used by the Mexican Indians, according to the Jesuit historian Acosta. In one of these ceremonies tamales, made of corn meal mixed with other foods, were blessed amid singing and beating of drums; having been transformed into the flesh of Tezcatlipoca by a process similar to transubstantiation, they were given to the children to eat, while the adults ate human flesh.

THE INCAS

A visit to Cuzco, in the Andes mountains in the south of Peru, and a study of the Inca Empire will convince anyone of the greatness of the civilization that came to an abrupt end through the conquest of Peru by Pizarro in 1532. In Cuzco, the capital of the Inca Empire, as well as in other old cities, ancient church buildings can be seen today with what seem to be solid stone foundations still standing, whose flimsy superstructures have crumbled with the destructive power of earthquakes and the erosive action of time. The foundations are the remains of Inca temples on which the Spaniards built their churches or monasteries in an attempt to eradicate the pagan religion. The mortarless Inca walls have defied the ravages of nature and time, while the Spanish structures crumbled and fell apart.

The spirit and much of the culture of this ancient people still remain in spite of conquest and oppression. The descendants of the Children of the Sun, whose mighty empire once numbered millions of people, and whose territory stretched from Ecuador to northern Argentina and Chile, are to be found today in the valleys and on the mountain slopes of the Andes, eking out a meager existence, surrounded by the monuments of ancient splendor.

The Inca civilization, like that of the Aztecs, came into being in a fertile valley. Cuzco, situated at 11,000 feet above sea level, lies in the center of one of the most productive valleys of Peru. The origin of the Inca civilization is, like the Aztec, surrounded by fables and legends, the most common of these being that the Sun took compassion on the benighted condition of the people of that region and sent two of his children, Manco Capac and Mama Ollo, to gather them into a community and teach them the arts of civilization. According to the legend, this pair, who were supposed to be both brother and sister and husband and wife, appeared on an island in Lake Titicaca carrying a golden wedge, and traveled northward until it suddenly sank into the ground and disappeared. This was the miracle and the sign; on that spot they established their abode. The people were impressed with their teachings, and soon the foundations of the city of Cuzco were laid.

It is generally assumed that the Incas first appeared around A.D. 1100. Theirs was not the only civilization that had flourished in the Andes before the Spaniards came; the Tiahuanaco, which covered most of the central highlands, whose great massive geometrical stone monuments are still standing, existed before the time of the Incas and disappeared about A.D. 900. Farther north, and prior to the Tiahuanacos, the Chavín culture developed in the highlands and, later, those of the Chimus and Nazcas on the coast of Peru.

One difficulty in piecing together the story of the Incas is that, unlike the Mayas, they left no permanent record and, therefore, what we know today of their culture and that of their predecessors is derived principally from two other sources. The first is the silent testimony of ruined or buried cities, temples and palaces, and the pottery and textiles found in huacas or burial grounds. The second is the story told by the early Spanish chroniclers, including viceroys such as Francisco de Toledo, and the writings of Garcilaso de la Vega, born in 1540, son of a Spanish father and an Inca princess.

The Incas resembled the Romans in that they had a genius for administration, statecraft, and colonization following military conquest. As Prescott puts it, " They proclaimed peace and civilization at the point of the sword." Thirteen Incas [4] reigned in splendor and magnificence over a period of four hundred years, until Atahualpa was overthrown by Pizarro in 1532 and the empire destroyed.

Though monogamy prevailed among the common people, the rulers themselves were polygamous, and a proud nobility was built up claiming descent from the same divine origin as the first Inca himself. The Inca, or emperor, as the representative of the Sun, stood at the head of the priesthood, and it was he who raised armies and commanded them; he ruled as a benign despot, making laws and providing for their execution. Thus both religious and political authority resided in the person of the Inca. His claims to power and ascendancy over the people of his vast empire were reinforced by the pomp and ceremony surrounding his person; his constant travels throughout his domain brought him into proximity with his subjects and further strengthened the quasi-divine image of the father-emperor. This portrayal was enhanced by the magnificence of the Inca's attire. The royal headgear was made of a turban of many colors with a scarlet tasseled fringe and two feathers from a rare bird found in the mountains. These birds were reserved exclusively for the Inca, and anyone found taking them or destroying them was put to death. Fresh fish and other foods were brought to the emperor's table in Cuzco from the coast of Peru by swift runners called *chásquis*.

The supreme authority of the Inca came down through many grades of officials, the lowest of whom supervised a group of ten families. The basic unit of Inca society was the ayllu or village community and, under the direction of the ayllu council, land was owned and cultivated communally. Private ownership, as we know it, did not exist. In each locality the land was divided into three parts: the first was cultivated for the Sun, the priests receiving the produce; the second portion went to the people, and the third was for the Incas, as rulers. The very young and the very old were exempted from manual labor. Goods were exchanged at great fairs on a barter basis, and the people knew neither the benefits nor the problems associated with money.

Agriculture flourished and was the mainstay of the economy. The descendants of the Incas still use the terrace method of cultivating the steep hillsides and the same primitive tools as their forefathers. Fish heads were used for fertilizing, as was also the guano brought from the islands off the coast of Peru, the natural habitat of the fish-eating birds of the Peruvian littoral.

The reign of the emperor Pachacutec from A.D. 1400 to 1448 marks the zenith of Inca power and empire. Pachacutec was not only an able administrator, he was also a noble philosopher. Here are some of his sayings which were passed on from father to son and recorded by the Spaniards:

> " Envy is a worm that gnaws and consumes the entrails of the envious."
>
> " Judges who secretly receive gifts from litigants ought to be looked upon as thieves and punished with death as such."
>
> " The noble and generous man is known by the patience he shows in adversity."

On one occasion, before an assembly of priests, Pachacutec stated that there must be some higher being than the sun, because it always follows the same path across the sky and it can be dimmed by any passing cloud. There must be a master or guiding hand which created all things, including the sun itself. These statements must have sounded like heresy to the priests who heard him.

Pachacutec conquered all the kingdoms along the Peruvian coast to the north; his son Tupac Yupanqui continued farther north and subdued a large part of what is now Ecuador in a unique maritime excursion. Thus the Inca Empire stretched for over a thousand miles from Chile to Ecuador. The next Inca, Huayna Capac, divided the empire between his sons Huáscar and Atahualpa. The forces of disruption had already set in, and civil war broke out. Atahualpa tried to seize the empire and later, while a prisoner of the Spaniards, had his half brother Huáscar killed. He, in turn, was put to death by the Spaniards in 1533.

The Inca Empire at the height of its power included many peoples subdued in amazing military campaigns over mountainous terrain, along the desert coast, and into the jungle, obstacles which previous cultures had been unable to surmount. Once the Incas had conquered a people, the process of spreading Inca culture and civilization began. Sometimes a tribe accustomed to Inca rule were moved to a newly conquered area; at other times the sons of headmen of conquered peoples were brought to Cuzco.

The splendor of the Inca Empire was enhanced by the colorful and elaborate pageants and religious ceremonies, sun worship being the most dignified and impressive of these. The best-known temple for the worship of the Sun was Coricancha, "the place of gold," in Cuzco. The interior of this temple was lavishly decorated with gold, and on the western wall there was a representation of the deity, in much the same way in which we sometimes personify the sun, with rays of light spreading in all directions. This figure was placed on a massive gold plaque encrusted with emeralds and other precious stones, and was so situated that as the sun came up in the morning its rays fell directly on it, lighting up the whole building, the shafts of light being reflected back by golden ornaments in walls and ceiling.

In addition to the main structure of Coricancha, there were several chapels, one of them being consecrated to the moon, which ranked second after the sun, and others to the stars. Cuzco was the mecca of the many tribes and peoples in the empire; although there were numerous other temples to the Sun in the provinces, none could compare in magnificence with Coricancha.

Next to the Inca came the high priest, chosen from among the members of the royal family and appointed for life. He in turn appointed other priests of a lower order who ministered in the temple and whose duties required them to be acquainted with all the ceremonies, feasts, and festivals, the four greatest of these coinciding with the solstices and equinoxes of the sun.

In the most important feast, namely, the feast of Raymi, a sacrifice of a llama was offered and its entrails examined in the search for favorable auguries. As part of the ceremony, a sacred flame was kindled and entrusted to the Virgins of the Sun. Bread made by these Virgins from maize flour was served along with fermented liquor at an elaborate feast presided over by the Inca himself and followed by dancing, drinking, and revelry which lasted for days. When the Spaniards came in the sixteenth century, they saw in the ceremony of distributing the bread and wine a striking resemblance to Holy Communion as practiced by the Roman Catholic Church. (This has been previously noted with reference to Aztec religious observances.) They also found a form of penance and confession which equally surprised them. The Spaniards had two explanations for these similarities: that the ceremonies were spurious and, therefore, the work of Satan, or that some early Christian teachers must have visited Peru in the past.

The Virgins of the Sun were young maidens specially chosen and trained for their religious duties, which required them to cut off all contact with the world. The Inca, or his wife, were the only ones who were allowed to enter the sacred precincts. The Virgins of the Sun employed their time spinning and weaving wearing apparel for the Inca and his royal household. Any Virgin discovered in an amorous affair was buried alive, her lover strangled, and his native village razed to the ground. The Virgins of the Sun were potential concubines of the Inca, the most beautiful being reserved for him. Hundreds of these maidens were accommodated in the royal palaces throughout the country. When any one of them was dispensed with, she usually returned to her home, where she was held in high regard and even reverence as the Inca's bride. Polygamy was practiced also by the nobles. Marriage among the common people was controlled to a certain extent by the government. No one could marry anyone outside his or her own community. On a given day all the marriageable young people were assembled in their local communities throughout the land and the marriage was performed by the *curacas* or headmen. Even in this personal matter of marriage, the government intervened. Prescott put it this way: " His very existence as an individual was absorbed in that of the community. His hopes and his fears, his joys and his sorrows . . . were all to be regulated by law. He was not allowed even to be happy in his own way." [5]

Although sun worship was the predominant feature of the religion of the ancient Peruvians and, as we have seen, it was closely related with the reigning Inca, who was believed to have descended directly from the Sun, they also worshiped lesser deities such as the thunder, the lightning, the rainbow, the elements, the winds, and the earth, as these were supposed to have some control over the existence of man. Similar to other Indian groups, they held a vague, undefined belief in a supreme being who was invisible and remote, but worship was generally confined to the perceptible manifestations of nature.

＊

The foregoing necessarily brief survey of the pre-Columbian religions in Latin America, laying the groundwork for an understanding of the present religious situation, cannot fail to impress us strongly with the fact that these three main systems offer further evidence of what history has so amply demonstrated: that a powerful sacerdotal class can fasten itself like an incubus upon the people, lending its moral sanction to oppressive governing groups or absolute rulers. Religion, in the sense in which we have used it, often means this. It neglects to minister to the soul of man and to satisfy his deep-seated needs. Only a dynamic faith based on the highest spiritual values can provide the power that sets man free and transforms society.

V

The Conquistadores
—Spain or God?

HISTORICAL PERSPECTIVE

History is not a series of isolated events belonging to the past; it is a continuum, and the present is its prolongation, an unfinished fabric, into which have been woven strands of many colors and varieties. The pattern of things at any given moment is largely the result of what has gone before. As the events of the past have played such an important part in the formation of Western culture, the religious situation in Latin America cannot be understood without a study of the forces that have contributed to make it what it is today.

In the previous chapter we have seen how religion permeated the life of the Indian peoples in the pre-Columbian era and the way in which the individual was subordinated to the community and the state and controlled by a priestly caste. The Spaniards and the Portuguese brought Roman Catholicism to the lands they conquered in the New World with a zeal and a success that have been rarely matched in history. Perhaps the fact that the native religions were of the fear-inspiring, idol-worshiping, and priest-dominated type made the change-over to Roman Catholicism, with its doctrine of hell-fire, its images and priests, not too difficult. The Roman Catholic Church has undoubtedly been the greatest single influence in the history of Latin America, its power being felt in every aspect of life, in the economic, social, and political spheres.

Until recently, popular writers on the culture and people of Latin America has seemed to avoid giving more than cursory attention to the religious situation. It is both significant and encouraging to note that in the last few years Roman Catholic writers, especially in the United States, have written with freshness and candor, not only about the present state of Roman Catholicism, but also about the way the church was first established in Latin America. There seems to be a new note of realism in approaching the subject.

In judging events of centuries ago, it is necessary to avoid doing so purely from a present-day point of view after a lapse of time has changed patterns of thought and values. We must try to appraise events in the light of mores and ideas prevalent at the time they took place, if not to justify them, at any rate to provide them with a rationale. The eminent Spanish writer Fernando de los Ríos urged that the Spanish colonial activities be judged not from the point of view of Catholics or Protestants, but from that of objective observers.[1]

Attention has already been drawn to the fact that in Latin countries in Europe — of which Spain was one — the authority of the Roman Catholic Church remained unshaken by the revolutionary impact of the Renaissance and the Reformation. We now wish to dwell on the particular problems and situations Spain was facing at the time.

No one will deny that the discovery of America in 1492 was one of those events which determine the course of history. The military conquest was but the prelude to one of the most dramatic crusades, one that was pursued with courage, devotion, ardor, and fanaticism, and one that produced both good and evil.

The Moors conquered Spain in 711 and occupied all but a small portion in the northwest of the peninsula. It is not without significance that the domination of that country by the Moors for nearly eight centuries came to an end in 1492, the year the New World was discovered. The Moslems were surprisingly tolerant of the Christians most of the time, offering them personal security and freedom of worship. The conquerors also made a great contribution to the arts, culture, industry, and agriculture of Spain. Many of the words in the Spanish language are of Arabic origin.

In the north of Spain, as time went on, the reconquest of their country took on the form of a crusade for the Spaniards, the rallying point and unifying force being the Roman Catholic Church. Hatred of the Moslems and an ardent love of Spain became a Christian as well as a patriotic duty. Thus there was created in Spain an idea or belief, which persists not only in Spain, but is quite strong in some Latin American countries, i.e., the identification of patriotism with Roman Catholicism.

In the fifteenth century the kingdoms of Castile and Aragon were united by the marriage of their sovereigns, Ferdinand and Isabella. The queen was a very devout Roman Catholic and is known in history as " Isabel la Católica." It was during her reign that religious unity became a political program and national unity a religious passion. This being so, the church itself had to be purged and purified, as well as the nation; Jews, Moslems, and dissenters were persecuted. The Inquisition was the chief instrument for achieving this unification. A royal edict created the Inquisition in Castile in 1477 and, after a papal bull confirmed it in 1483, it was accepted in Aragon the following year. The trial of heretics, their torture, the confiscation of property and death by burning, is a story written across the pages of history which needs no retelling here. In all fairness, however, it must not be forgotten that England has also been guilty of persecuting Catholics and expelling Jews, and that witch hunts have not been uncommon in that country and in New England.

Don Quixote and Sancho Panza

These two famous characters in the golden age of Spanish literature, Don Quixote and Sancho Panza, seem to represent twin aspects of the saga of the conquest and colonization of the New World. Quixote was the idealist, forever tilting at windmills; with a crusading spirit he set out passionately to right the wrongs of the world. With his lance and his eloquence he journeyed forth to restore the glories of a medieval world that had vanished, and to impose righteousness and justice upon all men. Don Quixote symbolizes the spiritual side of Spain's adventure in the New

World. Columbus' first voyage across the Atlantic was in some respects a spiritual undertaking, as it became a reality only after a series of disappointments, setbacks, and defeats, when he was able to secure the support of the devout queen even though two of her committees had turned the idea down. Columbus was a devout Catholic who was conscious that his given name meant " Christ bearer," and for him the adventure had religious undertones. However, as far as Spain was concerned, the real adventure began years after Columbus' first voyage of discovery, when the New World came within the purview of the Spanish people and the fabulous possibilities of that immense region dawned upon their consciousness.

The discovery, exploration, conquest, and settlement of the New World make one of the most brilliant chapters in imperial expansion ever known. Besides all this, however, the saga had all the characteristics of a great religious crusade with all the elements of daring, courage, mysticism, passion, and fanaticism. It seemed as though Spain was the chosen vessel of the Lord to carry out his designs in extending the boundaries of Christendom and winning new souls to the Roman Catholic faith.

Spain had just been unified politically, and the vast New World lay at its feet, like a prize for faithfulness and zeal. Forged on the anvil of eight centuries of struggle with the Moslems, Spain's religion was now of the proselytizing, virile type. Admirals, captains, and soldiers shared this religious fervor with the friars and priests who accompanied them on each expedition, and all were convinced that God was on their side. True to the strong individualism of the Spanish people, to which we have referred in a previous chapter, the conquistadores appropriated God for their great enterprise.

A spirit of adventure, of chivalry, daring, and heroic exploits had been engendered in the Spanish soul by the events and circumstances of history. The Roman Catholic faith had been vindicated and it must now be extended. The glory of Spain and of the Roman Catholic Church were one and the same thing. The motto on the standard of Hernán Cortés was: " Comrades, let us follow the sign of the holy cross with true faith, and through it we shall conquer." Inured to physical danger and hardship and lured on by visions of knightly honor and glory, soldier, adventurer, friar, and priest went forth in the spirit of Don Quixote de la Mancha, with a sacred fire burning in their souls.

The other side of the picture is represented by Sancho Panza, the arms bearer of Don Quixote. He was a realist, whose mind ran to food and money and the material things of life, and whose constant preoccupation it was to keep the saddlebags full. "You do not understand," replied Don Quixote. "I want you to know, Sancho, that honor demands that knights do not eat for a whole month . . . and if you had read as many stories as I have, in all of them you would find no reference at all to knights eating — except at some sumptuous banquet to which they were invited." Sancho Panza thus represents the material side of the conquest, and although we must be careful not to carry the simile too far, we would tend to agree with the following statement: " It would be wrong to picture the conquistadores as unadulterated Quixotes; the conquest years are replete also with evidences of the realistic Sancho Panza, eager for power and earthly lucre." [2]

THE WHITE LEGEND [3]

With the defeat of the Moslems in Spain in 1492, the reconquest of the country was complete and its golden age was ushered in. For the full details of this amazing story the reader will have to turn to other sources. What we are concerned with here is an attempt to understand the Spanish Conquest of America, the establishment of the Spanish American Empire, the introduction of the Roman Catholic faith, and the vast implications these tremendous events have had for the Latin American world of today.

Salvador de Madariaga maintains that the history of mankind can be divided into collective patterns, or historical entities, which he calls " bodies historic." [4] One of these is the Hispanic World. In the sixteenth century there began a great controversy over the nature of the conquest of Spanish America. This controversy, which began twenty years after the discovery of America, was, according to Mariano Picón y Salas,[5] whether the Conquest was a Christian crusade or, as Bartolomé de las Casas maintained, an enterprise of robbery and violence. The echoes of this conflict of opinion and interpretation have not died down yet; on the contrary, it has been very much revived in recent years. These differing points of view are known as the "White Legend" and the "Black Legend."

In two books published in 1947 [6] Madariaga makes an eloquent appeal for an understanding of the role of the Spaniard in the conquest of the New World. On the other hand we are indebted to Lewis Hanke, the eminent historian already mentioned,[7] for his painstaking research on the life and writings of Bartolomé de las Casas, stanch defender of the Indians against what he believed was cruel exploitation by the conquerors.

Madariaga has attempted to correct what he considers are some basic misconceptions and prejudices regarding the Spanish methods of conquest and colonization in the New World. He feels there is a universal prejudice against imperial Spain, and that in the Anglo-Saxon world Spain seems to be synonymous with oppression and cruelty, its chief symbol being the Holy Inquisition. Madariaga further believes that there are two reasons for the existence of these prejudices: one is that England, France, and Holland (and later the United States) had to blacken Spain in order to justify what they themselves were doing; the other, that Anglo-Saxons appear to have written far more about Spain than Spaniards have written about England.

There was a strange mixture of contradictory features in the character of the Spanish conquistador: unbelievable cruelty and greed on the one hand, and surprising generosity on the other; anarchy at one turn, and utmost fidelity to the king at another. Madariaga draws on his studies of the Spanish character (to which reference has been made in a previous chapter) in an attempt to explain these contradictions. The Spaniard is more true to character when serving either his own self or mankind; he "neglects the middle stretch, where grow the political, social, and municipal virtues." [8]

Title to the newly discovered regions was given to the monarchs of Spain by the pope in 1493 by a bull giving them absolute spiritual power over the people of the New World. The pope was considered to be the spiritual monarch of the universe. Thus the Catholic faith, which represented the universal, strengthened the individual conquistador in the carrying out of his heroic deeds, deeds that could involve cruelty or generosity, as the case may be. Madariaga tries to explain the acts of the Spanish conquerors by a polarization of the self and the whole, the individual and the universal.

In his thinking and writing Madariaga is always interesting and provocative; however, in endeavoring to counteract bias of judgment and interpretation of the forces at work in the rise and fall of the Spanish American Empire, he seems to weight his arguments in favor of his personal leanings. For instance, he says that Spain, faced with an entirely new and original situation, reacted as a state first and later in a Christian and magnanimous way. Recognizing the human problem in relation to the New World, Spain " officially adopted the most Christian and enlightened attitude toward the population of the New World." [9] He claims that the Christian spirit had won a magnificent victory in saving the Indians from slavery, and that Spain was ahead of the rest of the world in so doing. He condones the introduction of Negroes as slaves as the price that had to be paid for bringing into the Indies a new race to carry the burdens of serfdom.

In his defense of the Inquisition, Madariaga cites the trial and execution of Lambert in England on orders of King Henry VIII, the witch hunts in Germany, England, Scotland, Sweden, and New England, and observes that the Spanish Inquisition did not punish witchcraft with death. The Spanish Inquisition was founded in the first place — we are told — to discover Jews who had pretended to be converted to the Catholic faith, and was later applied to Protestants in an attempt to stamp out Protestantism in Spain. Madariaga denies that it was a dark institution designed to prevent the development of the human spirit. He maintains that that is a superstition held by some Protestants and freethinkers " which freethinking freethinkers should avoid." [10] Without realizing it, perhaps, Madariaga is here defending the principle that is a potent factor in the religious situation today, both in Spain and in Latin America, where the Roman Catholic Church claims to be the only true church and anyone who does not belong to it is in error. In other words, Madariaga would subscribe to the thesis so strongly defended by the Roman Catholic hierarchy today, that " error has no rights," error being that which does not conform to the dogma of the Roman Catholic Church.

A unique feature of Madariaga's justification of the Spanish Inquisition is his opinion that while the distortions of the history books have concentrated on its cruelties, they have neglected to highlight its true vice, which — he claims — was corruption. While the judgments were cruel and stupid, they were " on the whole, mild and progressive in relation to the standards of the period." [11] On the other hand, the Inquisition's chief crime was that it failed to uphold the very standards it professed to serve. Officials, high and low, became corrupt; " inquisitors speculated with the money of the Holy Office and waxed rich thereon, took mistresses, and dressed like young bloods in silk and lace." [12]

In 1569 Francisco de Toledo, Viceroy of Peru, stated that while ostensibly many monks and priests went to the New World to teach and indoctrinate the Indians, in actual fact they just enriched themselves at their expense.

When it comes to an examination of the historical record of the Roman Catholic Church in Spain, and particularly of its activities in the New World, Madariaga finds it difficult to avoid admitting that a serious deterioration set in during the course of time.

One of the strongest indictments is contained in a report of Ulloa and Jorge Juan, two scientists and naval officers who visited Peru between 1735 and 1740. They found that the friars and priests were exploiting the Indians, that most of them lived in open concubinage, and that the monasteries were public brothels. Other ecclesiastics lived a life of ease and luxury, while the Indians largely remained in serfdom and poverty. However, especially in the early days of the Conquest, some friars and priests had an apostolic zeal and an admirable spirit of sacrifice. Missionaries faced the perils and discomforts of journeys through the mountains and into the forests. Many of the higher secular clergy were known for their devotion to duty and for their exemplary lives.

BARTOLOMÉ DE LAS CASAS — HIS PLACE IN HISTORY

History books written both in Spanish and in English have given Bartolomé de las Casas a rightful place in history as the Apostle of the Indies, or the Defender of the Indians. It is probably true to say, however, that the profound significance of his work has not been fully recognized, nor is it too widely known. It is only recently that some of his writings have been published in English editions. Even so, writers of books on Latin America sometimes make scant reference to the work of de las Casas. A recent book running to over seven hundred pages devoted only four lines to this great figure.

Who was he, and how can his stature as an epic figure of the sixteenth century be measured? Did he merely have contemporary value, or did his life, thought, and action have significance for all time?

For sixty-four turbulent years out of his ninety-two on this earth, de las Casas was priest, conqueror, and colonist in the West Indies; reformer at the royal court in Spain; colonizer in Venezuela; friar in Spain and prelate in the New World; opponent of unjust wars against the Indians in Nicaragua; champion of justice in debates with other churchmen; promoter of a plan for Christianizing the Indians by pacific means; and successful advocate of the New Laws of the Indies.[13]

When Bartolomé de las Casas set out to write his famous *Historia General de las Indias,* he did so because, among other things, he believed that up to then all the historians dealing with the New World had been ignorant of the fact that " the new lands had been discovered principally as a means to Christianize their inhabitants," [14] and that the only justification for Spanish rule in the Americas was to bring the Indians to a knowledge of the

Christian faith. He became convinced that the early years of Spanish domination represented a great betrayal of that mission because the Spaniards were " carried away by blind lust for gold." [15]

To his detractors, de las Casas was a misguided fanatic and unreliable as a historian because, they maintained, his figures concerning the number of Indians killed by the Spaniards were exaggerated. They have considered him as the creator of the " Black Legend," which has provided ammunition for English, German, Dutch, and French writers who wished for sundry reasons to destroy the reputation of Spain. He had the distinction of being " the most hated man in America," [16] and even today imperialist Spain has not forgiven his accusations against it. To those who knew him best he was the great Defender of the Indians, the dominating figure of his time, and a truly Christian soul.

Lewis Hanke, who has had access to the original writings of de las Casas, highlights him as a historian, one of the most outstanding Spain has produced. [17] The results of Hanke's painstaking research in Spain on these writings have been made available in English and in Spanish.

Little is known of the details of de las Casas' family background, and most of what we know of his life is gleaned from his own writings. He was born in Seville in 1474, a descendant of the Casaus family, which originated in France. As a boy he probably heard tales of the exploits of his ancestors who took part in the conquest of the Canary Islands in the fifteenth century. His imagination was perhaps stirred by the news that the Turks had captured Constantinople and were already threatening Europe.

As a youth he studied in Salamanca, a university that in our time became the spiritual home of Miguel de Unamuno who, as the symbol of cultural freedom, represented the finest tradition of Spain. While Bartolomé was still a young man, his father Pedro accompanied Columbus on his second voyage to the New World and brought back an Indian boy as a slave for his son.

In 1502, ten years after Columbus' first voyage, Bartolomé de las Casas sailed to the New World as an adventurer and gentleman soldier. He settled in Hispaniola, or Santo Domingo; in payment for taking part in the occupation of the island, he was given an encomienda [18] of a hundred Indians, and he settled near the Arimao River. He exploited the Indians as the rest of his countrymen did, forcing them to labor in the mines and to do gold-washing in the rivers for his own enrichment.

DEFENDER OF THE INDIANS

De las Casas is known chiefly as the Defender of the Indians. In 1510, at the age of thirty-six, he was ordained a Roman Catholic priest, but evidently his conscience was still untroubled, for he continued his money-making enterprises based on the labor and enslavement of other human beings. It was not until the year 1514, when he was forty years old, that the great awakening came. Perhaps Friar Montesinos was responsible, more than anyone else, for this turning point in de las Casas' life. In 1512 he had heard Montesinos preach a sermon in which he thundered denunciations against the iniquities of the encomienda system, which produced many evils and injustices, chief of which was unpaid serf labor. Needless to say, Montesinos' courageous stand created much resentment and hatred among the colonists, including Padre de las Casas. As far as is known, Montesinos' was the first voice to be raised against the unjust treatment of the Indians in the New World. The Spanish colonists protested vigorously before the governor and sent a delegation to the Dominican monastery to threaten the expulsion of Montesinos from the colony. Far from being cowed by his visitors, the head of the monastery assured them that Montesinos had spoken for the Dominican Order; he promised, nevertheless, that the friar would preach the following Sunday on the same subject. The colonists left thinking they had won the battle. News of the expected retraction spread through the community, and prominent Spaniards flocked to hear it, but far from being any retraction, what they listened to was a further impassioned denunciation of the practices of the colonists.[19] A seed was thus sown in the heart and mind of de las Casas, a seed that was to germinate and develop into the most momentous decision of his life.

In 1514 he came across a verse in the Scriptures that greatly troubled him. During the Feast of Pentecost he was preparing a sermon when the Scripture lesson of the day burst in upon his mind with illuminating power. Reading from the Apocrypha (Ecclus., ch. 34), it was:

> He that sacrificeth a thing wrongfully gotten, his of-
> fering is ridiculous, and the gifts of unjust men
> are not accepted.
> The Most High is not pleased with the offerings of
> the wicked; neither is he pacified for sin by the
> multitude of sacrifices.
> Whoso bringeth an offering of the goods of the poor
> doeth as one that killeth the son before his fa-
> ther's eyes.
> The bread of the needy is their life; he that defraudeth
> him thereof is a man of blood.
> He that taketh away his neighbor's living slayeth him;
> and he that defraudeth the laborer of his hire is a
> bloodshedder.

For days de las Casas wrestled with these verses and their implications for his own life, until he became convinced of the error of his ways. Like Saul on the road to Damascus, his eyes were opened and the light of truth penetrated his whole being. This conversion experience was so real that he immediately gave up both his land and his Indians. With a new conviction burning within him, he preached a sermon in Sancti Spiritus in Cuba that caused as much consternation among the Spaniards as did that of Montesinos. The die had been cast, and henceforth he was to dedicate every waking thought, all his talents and energies, to denouncing, fighting, and seeking to remedy the gross injustice perpetrated against the Indians in the New World.

He began this great apostolate at the age of forty and continued for over half a century. It is not too much to say that, to a large extent, the struggle for justice for the Indians of the New World is the story of de las Casas' life and work, so monumental was his task and so closely did he identify himself with the cause to which he was committed. Some modern writers believe that in the life and work of de las Casas can be found the beginnings of the movement for freedom in the Americas, a movement that was to come to political fruition at the beginning of the nineteenth century. According to the Cuban writer Fernando Ortiz, " In Cuba, as in all the world, de las Casas is the first great apostle of liberty, in contrast to the merciless and sinister figures of the Conquest and colonization." [20]

While his main contributions are his writings and his advocacy of the cause of justice at the Spanish court and elsewhere, de las Casas sought earnestly to prove his main contentions and his thesis in deeds, i.e., in the realm of practice and not just theory.

Thus in 1521, seven years after his conversion, we see de las Casas as a colonist of a new type. His previous efforts within the encomienda system had meant ease and wealth for himself but poverty and misery for those who worked in serfdom for him. It was bad enough when he was an adventurer, as he was in the early years, but as a priest, engaged in this type of exploitation, there was bound to be a serious conflict between the Christianity he professed and the evil he practiced. He would now try a new method which did not violate his conscience, and one which he believed was the only Christian way to deal with the Indians. The project won royal approval and was put into practice in the north of what is now Venezuela; a region that was called *Tierra Firme*. Spanish farmers were recruited and sent out with farm implements and seeds to work the land alongside the Indians. They were to treat the Indian kindly and to seek to create a Christian community. It was hoped that the Indian, seeing the industriousness of the Spaniard, and being grateful for whatever advice and help he might receive, would turn naturally to the Christian faith, which he would not do if he were dispossessed of his land, separated from his family, and tyrannized.

De las Casas' plan, on the whole, was not unlike our modern efforts in rural missions. In those days it was a bold plan, as bold, says Lewis Hanke, as the circumnavigation of the globe by Magellan and the conquest of Mexico by Cortés.[21] The scheme was doomed to failure almost from the start, as any rural missions project would be if those who ran it did not have the right attitude and motivation. The Spaniards were not interested in the welfare of the Indians, nor in being merely tillers of the soil; rather, they were attracted by the possibility of wealth and position in the New World.

Following the failure of this colonization project, de las Casas entered the Dominican Order and retired to a monastery. It was ten years before he again took any active part in the affairs of the New World.

It is remarkable how de las Casas continued to hold to his conviction that the only way to convert the Indians to Christianity was by peaceful means, even in the light of his failure in *Tierra Firme*. His first important written work was called *The Only Method of Attracting All People to the True Faith,* which he produced in 1537.

In a sense, de las Casas was a precursor of the modern Protestant missionary movement, because his starting point was the great commission, "Go ye therefore, and teach all nations. . . ." He agreed with Pope Paul III that this mandate applied to the conversion of the Indians of the New World. He went farther and explained in his book the fundamental thesis that people can only be really won to the Christian faith by persuading them as rational beings who should be allowed to exercise their own free will. Faith, he claimed, comes from belief, and belief is based on understanding. Thus he felt it was both useless and unchristian to try to convert people to the Christian faith after you have robbed them, tyrannized over them, exploited them in forced labor, and oppressed them in every possible way.

Perhaps it was the writing of this treatise that led him to try another experiment in peaceful colonization. This time it was based in what is now Guatemala, and the project itself seems to have been more carefully conceived and carried out than the one in Venezuela; it was more successful and attracted wider attention. It was arranged with the governor of the mountainous province of Tuzutlán that any Indians converted under this project should not be turned over to Spaniards under the encomienda system, but that they should become subjects of the King of Spain voluntarily, and be under his special protection. Furthermore, it was agreed that for a period of five years only de las Casas and the other Dominican friars would be allowed to enter that area. De las Casas and his helpers began by composing ballads in the language of the people. These collections of verse ranged from the Creation of the world, through the Fall of man, to the life, miracles, and death of Jesus. Four Indian Christians were chosen, and they were taught these verses and how they should be sung. When the time came to initiate the program, de las Casas sent the Indians to the " Land of War " as traders. In the evening, to the accompaniment of weird musical instruments, they sang the rhymed couplets they had learned. They evidently delighted their audience, for they performed for eight successive nights, and when the Indians made it known they would like to learn more, the singers told them the friars were the only ones who could teach them. It was, therefore, agreed that the chief would send his brother to bring the friars in. It was decided to send only one friar at first, laden with gifts for the chief, who received him in royal fashion and granted him a special audience.

The chief ordered a church to be built and Mass to be said. He seems to have been favorably impressed by the cleanliness and good appearance of the friar compared with his own bedraggled, blood-stained priests. Inasmuch as his brother, whom he had sent on a mission to visit the friars, had found them to be as worthy as he had been led to believe, and because the governor had suspended the invasion of the province, the chief decided to become a Christian. He was the first convert to the Christian faith in that region which had been called *Tierra de Guerra* (Land of War) and was now called *Tierra de la Vera Paz* (Land of True Peace).

The experiment was enough of a success to prove to de las Casas that he was right in his approach to the Indians. The initial success was not followed up, however, largely because there were not enough Spaniards prepared to abandon the old methods of oppression, violence, and tyranny. It appears, notwithstanding, that some of the more oppressive Spanish governors were evidently convinced that this way of handling the Indians was not so unrealistic as it seemed at first.[22]

In 1542 the emperor Charles V promulgated the New Laws of the Indies, and it was generally agreed that this reform was due to the advocacy of de las Casas at the court. The laws were aimed at curbing the activities of the *encomenderos* and their exploitation of the Indians, but they failed largely in this attempt because the system was too deeply entrenched and the New World was far from Spain. Two years after the promulgation of the New Laws, de las Casas, apparently believing his cause had gained ascendancy in Spain, left for the New World, where he accepted the bishopric of Chiapas at the age of seventy. The following year the New Laws of the Indies were revoked by the emperor, and no further attempts were made by way of reform or of experimentation in new ways of pacific colonization.

In 1547 de las Casas resigned as bishop, returned to Spain, and spent the next nineteen years of his life writing treatises on the Indians and keeping in close touch with events and developments in the New World, making his personal influence felt in every possible way. Few men have shown such untiring and fearless devotion to a cause. From the time of his conversion until his death at the age of ninety-two, he spent half a century pouring out his life, his energy, and his talents in a passionate struggle for justice for an oppressed race. He not only wrote history, he made it, and thus became a unique and towering figure in the annals of the great Spanish people.

We shall now turn to a discussion of the thesis of de las Casas and the points of controversy that made him so famous.

THE STRUGGLE FOR JUSTICE

In his notable book on the life and work of de las Casas, Lewis Hanke characterizes him in three roles: political thinker, historian, and anthropologist.

His political thinking revolved around the validity of Spain's title to the New World regions. His leading question was: What makes Spain's dominion there legitimate? Montesinos, as early as 1511, had introduced this problem in his sermons. King Ferdinand of Spain was so disturbed by it that he commissioned several theologians to prepare a thesis in reply.

For a considerable time Portugal and Spain had been rivals for dominion over newly discovered lands. In 1469 the pope had settled some of the disputes, and in 1493, the year following Columbus' first voyage, Pope Alexander VI issued a bull granting absolute control to the king of Spain of all lands discovered by the Spaniards. The bull stated: " We give, concede, and assign them in perpetuity to you and the kings of Castile and of León, your heirs and successors; and we make, constitute and dispute you and your heirs and successors, the aforesaid lords of these lands, with free, full, and absolute power, authority, and jurisdiction." [23]

On his second voyage Columbus received his instructions, which contained the following: " The king and queen . . . desire nothing other than to augment the Christian religion, and to reduce many simple nations to the divine worship . . . , having more regard for the augmentation of the faith than for any other utility." [24]

The writings of the time are full of the idea that God had chosen Spain to bring the Christian religion to the New World.

De las Casas maintained that the pope had assigned the lands of the New World for one purpose only, that of Christianizing them, and he believed that everything else was a betrayal of that purpose and intent. He affirmed that the pope had only " voluntary jurisdiction " over non-Christians, by which he meant that the latter should not be forced to accept Christianity, but be persuaded to do so voluntarily. He further stated that he believed that the pope had no right to deprive non-Christians of their lands and goods, because all men were born free, and that individual freedom is something that comes from God. He would go only so far as to say that the pope could give authority to those who would Christianize the non-Christians, thus removing obstacles to such an end.

The debate aroused by de las Casas in his treatises and other writings was one that was widespread not only at the time, but was to continue for centuries, for it became a live issue again at the time of the independence movement at the beginning of the nineteenth century.

It has been generally considered that de las Casas was responsible for the introduction of Negro slaves into the New World, but modern writers increasingly deny the historical veracity of this charge against him. José A. Saco, the Cuban writer of the nineteenth century who more than anyone else was responsible for the publication of de las Casas' major work, *The History of the Indies,* maintains that it was the king of Spain and not de las Casas who introduced slavery into the New World.

During his lifetime de las Casas was the storm center of many disputes concerning the treatment of the Indians and the injustices perpetrated in the New World. The emperor Charles V called together a group of theologians and jurists, in what was known as a " congregation," to discuss these matters at Valladolid, in 1550–1551. The main point under discussion was whether it was legitimate for the Spaniards to " wage wars known as conquests " against the Indians in the New World if their only crime was that they were infidels. Such a controversy today would be laughed out of court in most circles, but it evidently aroused great interest in the sixteenth century, and the " congregation " attracted much attention. The two principal figures in the dispute were Dr. Juan Ginés de Sepúlveda, the king's Chronicler, and Padre de las Casas; both were eminent theologians and scholars. Sepúlveda was supported in his contention by men like the Archbishop of Tarragona, while de las Casas also had on his side some outstanding thinkers of the day, some of whom were greatly influenced by the famous Francisco de Vitoria, who also declared that the Spaniards had no right to be in the Indies at all, except for peaceful purposes such as trade and in order to convert the heathen to the Christian faith.

Sepúlveda justified the use of armed force against the Indians for the following reasons: their idolatry and other sins against nature; the rudeness of their minds, and their obligation to serve those of a more elegant mind, such as the Spaniards; and the fact that the Indians did harm to each other, sometimes killing one another. He claimed that if they were subjected first, it would be easier to preach the Christian faith to them afterward.

The argument which de las Casas refuted more than any other was that certain individuals are slaves by nature, which was the Aristotelian idea. He proclaimed his conviction that the Indians of the New World were neither slaves by nature nor stupid creatures of limited understanding, but men who would embrace the Christian faith of their own free choice if given a chance.

It is to the credit of sixteenth-century Spain that in the dispute at Valladolid the ideas of de las Casas prevailed, and that there were many men like him who believed in these basic principles of justice. Modern Latin American writers consider de las Casas and like-minded Spaniards of his day as the true Spaniards, rather than those who believed, like Sepúlveda, that the Indians were inferior and should be treated harshly.

De las Casas stood for a doctrine that was valid not only in his day, but is timeless; it has profound implications for our contemporary world as we face the complex problems of race and underdeveloped peoples.

This good man put his duty to God first and service to the king afterward; Sepúlveda served the emperor first and the church took second place. Fernando Ortiz says that Sepúlveda was with those " at the top " and de las Casas with the underdog; Sepúlveda was what we would call today a " rightist " and a conservative, while de las Casas was more of a " leftist " and a reformer.[25]

We have said that de las Casas was a notable historian; perhaps his monumental work, *Historia General de las Indias,* which he wrote over a period of nearly forty years, was his outstanding contribution to the cause of justice and to the Latin American world. In it can be seen evidences of a passion to record the truth of events and the sweep of history, of which he himself was a part. For a long time to come, historians and writers will go to this work for inspiration and information regarding the greatest event in modern history, the discovery and conquest of the New World.

During the closing weeks of his long life, in 1566, de las Casas wrote: " I believe that because of those impious and ignominious acts, perpetrated unjustly, tyrannously, and barbarously upon them [the Indians], God will visit his wrath and ire upon Spain for her share, great or small, in the bloodstained riches obtained by theft and usurpation, accompanied by such slaughter and annihilation of these people, unless she does much penance."

Thus this Spaniard devoted his life, energies, and talents to the cause of the Indians of the New World and to the proposition that true Christianity cannot be spread by conquest, but only by " the methods of Christ." He was one of the principal actors in the great drama of the New World of the sixteenth century, a drama full of adventure, glory, heroism, violence, pain, and suffering, the elements of which determined in large measure the subsequent sociological, political, and religious patterns of the Latin America we know today. What began in 1493 ostensibly as an assignment of lands by the pope in order that the people might be Christianized, became a conquest, the character of which was more ruthless because of its fanatical religious zeal.

By and large, the underlying motives in the conversion of the Indians of the Spanish territories in the New World were not, except in rare cases, the spiritual redemption and happiness of these people, but to make them subjects, or vassals, of the Spanish king. Thus a large part of the Americas became a Spanish empire, in the establishment of which a crusading, intolerant religion was the handmaiden rather than the great determining influence.

The gospel of Jesus Christ as a transforming and redeeming power in individual lives and in society did not reach the shores of Latin America; instead, a militant, inflexible religion came as part of a conquering force, and a legion of ruthless men, imposing their will on largely defenseless natives, ostensibly did so for the glory of God, which meant the glory of Spain.

VI

From Paganism
to Roman Catholicism

In the name of the Prince of Peace they ratified a contract of which plunder and bloodshed were the objects." [1] With these words the historian Robertson described the famous pact or covenant entered into by Pizarro, Almagro, and Luque in Panama on March 10, 1526. The first two were the commanders of the expedition that was to conquer Peru, and Luque was the priest who furnished the twenty thousand pesos for the undertaking. Scant mention is made in the history books, however, of the fact that Luque was the representative of Licentiate Gaspar de Espinosa, of Panama, who really contributed the funds.

The signing of this famous pact and the taking of an oath provided a very solemn occasion. The document began by invoking the Holy Trinity and the Blessed Virgin, and went on to state that the parties to the pact had full authority to discover and subdue the lands lying to the south of the Gulf of Panama, namely, the Empire of Peru, and that each signer of the pact would be entitled to one third of the lands, treasures, gold, silver, et cetera, as well as one third of all the vassals, rents, and emoluments that might be conferred by the crown.

The historian W. H. Prescott tends to minimize the striking contrast between the rapaciousness and inhumanity of the parties to the pact on the one hand, and the deeply religious tone and spirit of the occasion on the other, by pointing out that we must take into account the spirit of the times. It is our conviction, however, that religion, and especially Christianity, cannot become an accomplice of conquest by lending moral sanction to it, without identifying itself to some extent with the injustice and cruelty implicit in such an undertaking. The use of force and violence must forever be alien to the basic Christian teachings and cannot be reconciled with them.

THE CONVERSION OF ATAHUALPA

We shall attempt now a discussion of the kind of religion the Spaniards brought to the New World, and shall try — in this and the next chapter — to describe the religious conditions to which it gave rise in Latin America. The divorce between religion and life that is characteristic of the culture of Latin America today may be seen from the early days of the Conquest.

In 1532, the year after the Pact of Panama, careful preparations were made by the Spaniards for the capture of the Inca Atahualpa, by deceit and treachery, in the main square of Cajamarca, a city in the north of Peru. Spanish infantry and cavalry were placed strategically around the plaza so that when the Inca arrived with his retinue they might capture him by surprise. After putting their arms in good order and placing bells on the breastplates of their horses with the idea of creating confusion among the Indians, Mass was celebrated with great solemnity by the soldiers. The blessing of God was invoked as a protecting shield around them as they joined in the chant *" Exsurge, Domine "* (Rise, O Lord, and judge thine own cause). One would almost have imagined them to be a group of martyrs ready to lay down their lives for their faith, rather than a band of licentious adventurers " meditating one of the most atrocious acts of perfidy on the record of history."[2]

Having been previously assured by the Spaniards that he would be received as a friend and a brother, Atahualpa decided to leave the main body of his troops behind and enter the plaza with only a few unarmed warriors to accept the hospitality offered him. This the Spaniards took to be an indication that Providence favored their scheme.

The sun was about to set over the hills surrounding Cajamarca when the royal procession reached the gates of the city. An advance group of servants arrived to clear the path for the Inca; these were followed by noblemen and guards impressively attired in multicolored garments and uniforms. In the melancholy twilight the royal procession entered the square, holding aloft on a golden throne the mighty ruler of the Inca Empire. Five or six thousand people followed the procession and, as it came to a halt, silence fell upon the multitude. There was an air of expectancy as the Inca inquired about the location of the strangers. Little did he realize that this was a fateful moment in the history of his empire.

At that moment a Dominican friar, Vicente de Valverde, emerged from the gloom of the surrounding buildings with a Bible in one hand (or, according to some authorities, a breviary) and a crucifix in the other, and approached the Inca. Through an interpreter named Filipillo, Valverde began by expounding the doctrine of the Trinity, and continued on through the creation of man and his Fall to the act of redemption by Christ through his crucifixion and ascension, and how he had left the apostle Peter as his vice-regent on earth. He stated that the successors of Peter had power over all potentates here below, and one of them had commissioned the Spanish king to conquer and convert the natives of the Western Hemisphere. The friar, therefore, called upon the emperor to abjure his own false faith and to embrace Christianity.

In the translation, Filipillo told the Inca that " the Christians believed in three gods and one God, and that made four." [3] What the Inca seemed to understand well enough, however, was that he was supposed to acknowledge the supremacy of the king of Spain. He replied with considerable indignation that he would be tributary to no man, and that as for the pope giving away lands that did not belong to him, he must have been out of his mind. With regard to the Christians' religion, he said he could not accept it, since he believed in a god (the Sun) who reappeared every morning, whereas the Christians' God was put to death by the men he created.

When asked by what authority he spoke, Valverde pointed to

the book in his hand and offered it to Atahualpa. As he took it, the Inca must have suddenly realized the full import of what was happening, for he threw it down in anger and demanded that the Spaniards give complete satisfaction for all the wrongs committed in his land. Thereupon the friar urged Pizarro to give the signal for the attack rather than " wasting our breath in talking with this dog." He added: " Set on at once. I absolve you." [4]

In the furious assault that followed, thousands of defenseless Indians fell, while only one Spaniard was hurt and that was Pizarro himself, wounded in the arm by one of his own men while defending the Inca from a blow, since he wished to capture him alive. That night Pizarro bade his men offer thanks to God for the miracle he had wrought. Subsequent events proved that the capture of the Inca was the deciding factor in the conquest of Peru.

The rest of the story, of the ransom amounting to the equivalent of several million dollars' worth of objects of gold assembled by the Inca's subjects, and the eventual execution of the Inca on trumped-up charges, is well known. Years later, as if by an inexorable justice, Almagro, who had entered into the solemn pact at Panama with Pizarro, was executed by order of the latter; and Pizarro himself was killed by his own men in the palace in Lima.

RELIGION AND POLITICS

In the minds of the Spaniards of the sixteenth century there was a close connection between theology and the legal claims of Spain to conquered lands. An extraordinary theory had developed over the centuries, beginning with the writings of Henry of Susa, cardinal bishop of Ostia. It was his contention that before the time of Christ heathen people were entitled to their own political jurisdiction and possessions, but that with the coming of Christ all these powers and rights passed to him. Christ was Lord of the earth, and he had delegated his supreme dominion, both spiritual and temporal, to Peter and his successors, the popes. This theory was used to justify the Conquest of the New World, and it explains the tremendous importance attached to the papal bull of

1493, ceding New World territories to the king of Spain. It gave rise also to the *requerimiento,* which was the substance of Friar Valverde's address to Atahualpa. The *requerimiento* was written by a jurist named Juan López de Palacios Rubios and, based on the theory just referred to, its purport was to establish the right of the Spaniards to dominate the lands of the heathen. It "expounded the doctrine of the division of the world into Christian and heathen, and stated the right of Christ through his representative, the pope, to hold the infidel world in subjugation." [5]

The document refers to the creation of the world in accordance with the Bible account, and states that Christ chose Peter as his vicar and commanded that he be seated in Rome "as the fittest place for governing the world." The document then moves on to political considerations, stating that Pope Alexander VI had given all the isles and mainland to the Catholic rulers of Spain.

Every Spanish conquistador was required to have the *requerimiento* read to the Indians by a notary and through an interpreter, before seizing any of their territory. The military commander usually sent a report back to Spain with the required signatures; probably by doing so he cleared his conscience of any feeling of guilt.

In parenthesis it can be said that this procedure exemplifies some typical psychological traits of the Spaniards which are to be found among Latin American people today, and to which reference has already been made. The act of reading the *requerimiento,* and the fact that it had to be read by a notary, demonstrate the extreme formality and juridical sense of the Spanish character.

After the *requerimiento* was read to the Indians, they were given time to think things over. Among all the theological and political considerations and implications, three points stood out: The Indians were called upon to acknowledge the Roman Catholic Church as mistress of the world, they were to recognize the pope as its head, and they were to accept the king of Spain as their ruler in place of their own. If they accepted these conditions, they would be given many privileges; and if they also wished to be converted to the Christian faith, then the king would show them many favors. If they resisted these offers, their lands would be occupied and their possessions taken, the people would be subdued " by the help of God," and their wives and children would also become slaves.

The closing sentence of the *requerimiento* left very little choice in the matter in spite of the grandiloquent phrases and promises. It said, " And I protest that all the death and destruction which may come from this is your own fault, and not His Majesty's, or mine, or that of my men." [6]

Thus there was established in Latin America the pattern of a close relationship between religion and politics, a relationship that those who have lived only in other countries find it difficult to understand.

Ever since the time of the Conquest, the church and the state have been united. In modern times some countries have found it necessary to separate them because of the abuses and evils that have arisen. The church has used the state to enhance its own power and prestige, while the state has used the church as a means of social control and as a political weapon. Clericalism [7] has been the bane of political life in Latin America. Supported by the church, dictators have wielded tyrannical power over the people, and some do so even today. Nowhere else in the world can the evil effects of clericalism be seen so manifestly as in Latin America. Moreover, clericalism has given rise to anticlericalism, and this antagonism has often erupted in violence and bloodshed, as in Mexico.

The Dogmatic Approach

Valverde's address to Atahualpa, as well as the *requerimiento,* embodied a pronounced dogmatism which was accepted with very little questioning or reasoning by the Spaniard and imposed on others in the same spirit. The Indians were not supposed to dispute any of the teachings of the priests or friars; all they were expected to do was accept them and learn by rote the prayers, the catechism, and the creed.

Once the peoples of the New World were conquered and sub-dued, the church was faced with the colossal task of depaganizing them. How was the Christian religion to be communicated to people of a totally different culture and background? This is a problem that Christian missionaries have faced over and over again in many different places across the world, and the answer is by no means simple. The apostle Paul met this very situation on his missionary journeys, and his approach was usually an appeal to reason, either in his manner of presentation or by answering questions. He often began his dissertation at a point familiar to his hearers, as he did on Mars Hill, where he said: " Ye men of Athens, I perceive that in all things ye are too superstitious. For as I passed by, and beheld your devotions, I found an altar with this inscription, TO THE UNKNOWN GOD. Whom therefore ye ignorantly worship, him declare I unto you " (Acts 17:22-23).

One set of circumstances seemed to help in the conversion of the Indians to Christianity, and to this we have already referred: there was an extraordinary resemblance between certain aspects of the pagan religions and Christian beliefs and practices. Among these were Communion, Baptism, confession, penance, and belief in immortality. The use of the cross and of shrines was also com-mon among some Indian tribes.

As part of the effort to Christianize the natives, the Spaniards established what were called *reducciones,* or villages into which the Indians were brought for labor and instruction. Industrial schools were set up in which they were taught masonry, carpen-try, and the crafts, and they worked as laborers on the surround-ing land, in the cultivation of the soil or in husbandry. Schools were established under the aegis of the church, but while the re-ligious indoctrination was thorough, the education given was very rudimentary.

The work of Christianizing the Indians was carried on mainly through the missionary work that began in 1493 in the Caribbean area with the arrival of twelve friars who accompanied Columbus on his second voyage. The most famous mission was the one es-tablished in Paraguay among the Guarani Indians, called La Plata

Mission. Beginning in 1608, it had become a major enterprise by the middle of the eighteenth century, with 30,000 Indians living in neighboring villages. With the expulsion of the Jesuits in 1767, the work was taken over by the Franciscans. The mission was ruled by the Jesuits with benevolent paternalism, but it was also a despotic rule, and the Indian was kept under rigid discipline and control. His work in the fields produced crops of cotton, tobacco, and yerba maté, and helped fill the mission treasury. He was given regular religious instruction and also allowed to indulge in pageantry and games.

The Indian's wants were largely cared for, but this relative security was offset by a submissiveness, docility, and complete lack of training for civic responsibilities in economic and political life. The Indian was not supposed to bother about such things; his physical needs were more or less met and he was now a good Christian. As Hubert Herring puts it: " He had no practice in self-government, no responsibility for his economic life, and small opportunity to learn new skills." [8]

It is believed that the first formal presentation of Christianity in South America was Valverde's address to Atahualpa; in that sermon there was an underlying assumption that once the tenets of Christian theology were outlined, even though the terms of reference were entirely foreign to the hearer, he had no choice but to accept.

The very ease with which the Indian seemed to accept the Roman Catholic religion meant that for him it was both meaningless and sterile. The passivity of the Indian facilitated his catechization, but did not help his understanding of doctrine, belief, or practice. We shall refer later on to his reaction and to other factors that lay behind his ready acceptance of Roman Catholicism.

OUTWARD CONFORMITY

Following his capture by the Spaniards, " it was not long before Atahualpa discovered, amidst all the show of religious zeal of his conquerors, a lurking appetite more potent in their bosoms

than either religion or ambition. This was their love of gold." [9]
Orders went out from the Inca's prison that his subjects should
bring objects of gold with which he had promised to fill the room
in which he was confined, and which were to be his ransom. In
the meantime, Valverde labored hard to convert Atahualpa to the
Christian faith, but to no avail. Afraid of the intrigues of his half
brother Huáscar, with whom he shared the Inca Empire, Atahualpa ordered his death by drowning. In 1533, Atahualpa was
brought to trial and sentenced to be burned alive in the main
square of the city of Cajamarca. In one final exhortation, with
the fagots already around the unfortunate victim, Valverde made
a last appeal to him to abjure his false faith, become a Christian,
and thus save his soul. Informed that if he did so his sentence
would be changed to death by strangling, Atahualpa consented
and was baptized John, in honor of John the Baptist, on whose
day the event took place.

What Valverde was unable to do by means of his sermons he
accomplished when the victim faced the horrors of death by
burning. An outward assent was all that was necessary. On the
other hand, the priest was true to the belief of his church that the
soul must be saved even if it meant destroying the body. The Indian was willing to go through the motions of an acceptance of
the faith so persistently presented to him, even though he failed
to understand the meaning of the new forms of worship. He soon
found that an outward conformity was all that was required.

One of the tragedies of Latin America today is the continued
outward religious observance, without the inward transformation
of the individual, a radical change of values, and a commitment of
life to Christ.

The "Christianization" of the Indian

It has been pointed out that the Spaniards embarked upon what
can be called a religious crusade in the New World, and that their
drive for the conversion of the natives to Christianity closely followed — although in the case of some individuals it overtook —
their overweening ambition for conquest and material gains. To

achieve this end they spared no effort. We shall now study the ways, often subtle and hidden, in which the Indians defeated the intent of the Spaniards to Christianize them.

The nominal conversion of the Indians to the Roman Catholic religion was consummated with relative ease; in fact, the success of the early missionaries seems to have been phenomenal. Indians were baptized by the thousands, and if the missionaries could not go to them, they came long distances to receive baptism. Some were even baptized over and over again because they thought this would please the Spaniards. Often the priests were unable to cope with the demand for baptism. As early as 1531, Bishop Zumárraga reported that the Franciscans alone had baptized at least a million and a half people.

The Franciscans simplified the ritual of baptism because the number of Indians who came was so great and the number of missionaries prepared to baptize so insufficient. Motolinía refers to a certain monastery called Quecholac in Mexico, to which great numbers of Indians came seeking baptism — the young, the aged, the healthy, and the sick. Writing to a colleague, he said, " I tell you that in five days that I was in the monastery, another priest and I baptized about 14,200, putting on each one the holy oil and chrism, all of which was no light task." [10]

Historians have adduced a number of reasons why the people were so easily converted to Catholicism. Some believe the docility and passivity of the Indian was one factor; others point to the similarity of practices in the religions of the Indians and that of the Spaniards, while one writer quotes an Indian chief as saying the Indians were weary and dissatisfied with the requirements of their own religions.

Some writers point out, on the other hand, the factors that hindered conversion: the evil example of many Spaniards, their gross mistreatment of the natives, and the low moral character of many priests.

In many instances the conversion of the Indian was nominal, and " as long as the Indians confessed to be Christians and baptized their children in the church, the Catholic priests made no exclusive demands on their consciences." [11]

By and large, the principal aim of the Spanish friars, priests, and missionaries seems to have been to proselytize rather than to evangelize the Indians. Not only was the task of baptizing the Indians so formidable that little time was available for indoctrination of the new converts, but the Spaniards also recognized the limitations of the Indians and very early abandoned any attempt at explanation or discussion of theology or doctrine. The Indian undoubtedly understood very little of the content of his new religion.

THE "ACCOMMODATION" OF ROMAN CATHOLICISM

Another important factor in the facility with which the new religion was accepted by the Indians was the way in which it accommodated or adapted itself to their religious ideas and practices in order to allow the Indians to feel more at home in the new religion. For example, it was the custom of the Spanish priests to select deliberately for the building of a Christian church the site on which the Indians had been accustomed to worship their own gods. Two noted examples are the Roman Catholic cathedrals in Mexico City and Cuzco, Aztec and Inca capitals. The Spaniards believed this practice would facilitate the transition from paganism to Christianity; what they did not realize was the subtle way in which the Indian hereby was able to keep alive his own religion. According to the noted Mexican writer Alberto Rembao: "Accommodation was inevitable in view of the fact that the Indian soul was, and is, a very potent soul, and that the potency sprang from its religion; religion and soul were identical and in order to preserve the one, the other must be maintained as well." [12]

The same accommodation or easy transition was made in the continuation of the Indian *fiestas*. The Roman Catholic priests did not try to abolish the Indian feast days. They just organized Roman Catholic feast days to coincide with the dates of the traditional Indian festivals. "The pagan ecstasy was simply converted to Christianity by the addition of a saint's day, a Mass, and a benediction. . . . So now in the name of San Juan (John the Baptist), the Indians of northern Ecuador sweep down from the hills, drink *chicha* for five days and nights, fill the air with their plaintive, haunting flutes, and dance and weep and fight." [13]

Dr. Rembao maintains that the Indians were metaphysicians because for them the idol was not a god but the image of an invisible god. To the Mexican Indian his gods were real; they were spiritual beings with whom he communicated and, as such, the gods were able to survive the destruction of both images and temples. So the Indian continued to believe in the existence of his gods, and when the Spaniard brought his Christian images of the Virgin, of Christ, and of the saints, these images began to acquire virtue just the same as the pagan idols had. " Here we see conquest in reverse: the Christian saint is impregnated with the spirit of the pagan idol." [14]

The Indian is still a metaphysician. While in the south of Peru, the writer noticed an image of Christ on the cross in a certain church. His attention was called to the pieces of broken mirror in the crown of thorns. They had been placed there for a purpose. What could it be? An anthropologist from the United States, who had spent several months studying Indian life and customs, gave his explanation. He said the Indians put these little mirrors in the image so that they might catch the rays of the sun; thus, while they worshiped the image as good Roman Catholics, at the same time they were worshiping the sun, as their ancestors had done.

We have referred to the way in which the Spaniards attempted to accommodate their religion to that of the Indian by building their churches on the site of the teocallis, or pagan temples, which they had destroyed. As part of the substitution process, the Indians were set to work to build the churches. In many instances they surreptitiously used their own stone idols as foundation stones, cornerstones, or pillars of the church. Fray Jacinto de la Serna interprets such a stratagem as a ruse of the devil to deceive the Indians, " so that they could say that their gods were so strong that they were put as foundations and cornerstones of temples." [15]

The Transfer of Deities

The transfer of deities can be seen in a most striking way in the origin of the famous shrine of Our Lady of Guadalupe on the outskirts of Mexico City. In 1531, just twelve years after Cortés had conquered Mexico, the Virgin appeared to Juan Diego, a fifty-five-year-old Indian, who was hurrying down Tepeyac Hill to hear Mass in Mexico City. The story of how the Blessed Virgin told Juan Diego to go to the bishop and persuade him to build a temple on the spot where she stood on Tepeyac Hill is well known. We are told that when the bishop bade him ask for a sign, Juan Diego went back to the hill, and the Virgin sent him to a rock where he found some beautiful Castilian roses, blooming out of season. Returning to the presence of Bishop Zumárraga, the Indian opened his cloak, and the roses fell out before him. Moreover, at that moment a life-sized picture of the Virgin appeared on the Indian's cloak; this picture can be seen today in the great Basilica of Our Lady of Guadalupe.

It is interesting to note that not only is the Virgin of Guadalupe of very dark complexion, but the story about her appearance relates that she spoke to Juan Diego in the Aztec language and that she was dressed in native garb.

Father Bernardino Sahagún made a further observation: that the Virgin appeared to Juan Diego on the hill where the shrine of Tonantzín had been. He says: "In this place they had a temple dedicated to the mother of the gods, whom they called Tonantzín, which means 'our mother.' There they made many sacrifices in her honor . . . and men, women, and children attended the festivals. . . . Now the church built there is to Our Lady of Guadalupe." [16]

In his anthropological studies in Tepoztlán, fifty miles from Mexico City, Oscar Lewis found many evidences of the fusion of the Aztec and Catholic religions. For instance, in the figure of Tepoztecatl, a culture hero who became an Aztec god, he found old Aztec concepts had been mixed with those of Catholicism. "His figure is also fused with the god Ometochtli, so that today he is known as El Tepozteco, god of the wind and son of the Virgin Mary. For Tepoztecans, the Catholic Trinity is viewed as a combination of three distinct gods, and the cross is a magical symbol which has no relation to the death of Jesus. Tepoztecans continue to fear omens, evil spirits, and *los aires*. When they are in dire need of rain, they pray to El Tepozteco for aid." [17]

During a visit to the Peruvian Andes in 1928, Julio Navarro Monzó observed a rough cross of stone with a crude figure of Christ on it. At the foot of the cross were some flowers and an earthen vessel containing liquor, placed there by the Indians. In Lima he discussed this with some Peruvian writers and artists. Navarro Monzó expressed the opinion that these crosses, frequently found on the wayside in the Peruvian sierra, reminded the Indian of the fundamental fact of the death of Jesus as the Savior of mankind. He was promptly contradicted by the group. One of them said: " You are mistaken. Those crosses do not remind the Indians of any such thing. The first missionaries who came to this continent destroyed the idols the Indians worshiped and told them that instead they should worship those crosses. More or less quietly the Indians accepted this fact and they continue to lay before the cross the same offerings they had set before Pacha-Mama, Pacha-Kamac, and Wira-Cocha, with a similar object and for identical reasons as before, namely, to ask the unknown supernatural forces to protect them from danger, to withhold their anger, to give them prosperity, and to leave them in peace. That is all. Of Christianity the Indians know today about as much as their ancestors knew before the Spaniards came." Navarro Monzó continued: " Of the Carpenter, the Man of Nazareth, they only have a vague idea. Of his teachings they know nothing." [18]

MIRACLE, MYSTERY, AND AUTHORITY

In his immortal novel *The Brothers Karamazov*, Dostoevsky has dramatized some of the characteristics of sixteenth-century Spanish Catholicism in the chapter called " The Grand Inquisitor." The scene is laid in Spain " in the most terrible time of the

Inquisition, when fires were lighted every day to the glory of God." According to the story, Christ appeared in the streets of Seville the day after a hundred heretics had been burned by order of the cardinal "in the presence of the king, the court, the knights, the cardinals, the most charming ladies of the court, and the whole population of Seville." [19] Christ came unobserved, but everyone seemed to be aware of his presence and to be drawn to him irresistibly; they flocked to him and followed him; they brought the lame and sick, and he raised a child from the dead. At that moment the cardinal, the Grand Inquisitor, an old man of nearly ninety years of age, passed by, saw what was happening, and ordered the guards to seize Christ and cast him into prison.

The cardinal then visits Christ in prison, stealthily, in the dead of night, and carries on a one-sided conversation, as Jesus never once replies. "Why art Thou come to hinder us?" he asks. "To-morrow I shall condemn Thee and burn Thee at the stake as the worst of heretics." Perhaps there was no need for Christ to come then at all, for "all has been given by Thee to the pope and all, therefore, is still in the pope's hands." [20] The Grand Inquisitor then proceeds to discuss the question of freedom. "Didst Thou not often say, then, 'I will make you free'? For fifteen centuries we have been wrestling with Thy freedom, but now it is ended and over for good. . . . Thou hast given us the right to bind and unbind." [21]

This leads to a discussion of the three temptations of Jesus in the wilderness. The cardinal maintains that the whole subsequent history of mankind is summed up in the three questions involved. "There are three powers," he says, "and three powers alone, able to conquer and to hold captive forever the conscience of these impotent rebels for their happiness. Those forces are Miracle, Mystery, and Authority. Thou has rejected all three," he tells Christ. After a lengthy discussion of these three forces, the Grand Inquisitor says, "We have corrected Thy work and have founded it upon Miracle, Mystery, and Authority." [22]

Dostoevsky's thinking in this chapter, "The Grand Inquisitor," is very profound, as profound as the subject of freedom itself. The religion that the Spaniards took to Latin America was not based on freedom, individual freedom, the freedom to which Paul referred when he said: "Stand fast therefore in the liberty wherewith Christ hath made us free," but rather it is a religion based on Miracle, Mystery, and Authority. The whole idea of a free individual whose life is yet disciplined under God because it has been freely committed to him was something entirely foreign to the Roman Catholic conquistadores of the sixteenth century.

Miracle, Mystery, and Authority, all helped produce in Latin America a religion that demands little thought and invites no questions, a body of concepts and ideas that had to be accepted and not discussed. In most cases the Indian of the New World was overawed. His experience was no match for the combined weight of Miracle, Mystery, and Authority in the hands of the priests. That is why religion for him became largely an attitude of extreme reverence and veneration, for he felt that he would do well to be on good terms with the Being behind all this. At the same time, as we have seen, there was nothing incongruous in his continuing to believe in, and worship, the gods of his fathers in whatever ways he was able to.

THE CHRIST OF LATIN AMERICA

The spiritual life and ethical conduct of people are determined not so much by the fact that they worship God, but by the kind of God they worship. It is important to try to understand the kind of Christ brought to the New World, and to inquire what was the commonly held view of him. The religious conditions in Latin America today are largely a consequence of the place Christ has held from the beginning. Was he the living, risen Christ we know through the pages of the New Testament, or was he another? In his remarkable book *The Invisible Christ,* Ricardo Rojas describes his conversations with a Roman Catholic bishop in Argentina. Rojas is seeking an authentic picture of Christ, the real Christ. He tells the bishop: "I have in my collection of images of Christ a crucifix of wood which I acquired in Spain and which is probably the work of some convert on the Moorish frontier in the sixteenth century. The figure of the Christ on this crucifix is that of a mulatto. . . . We have an Indian [native] Christ, and this comforts me, since in the three Wise Men who worshiped Jesus in Bethlehem, only the three races of the continents known at that time are represented. There was lacking in that court the copper-colored king, the Inca of America. Fifteen centuries later the man from America reached Bethlehem." [23]

In the preface to his book, Ricardo Rojas explains that an old painting he had in his possession was the starting point for his first discussion with the bishop. " The canvas represents the Holy Trinity in the attitude of crowning the Virgin, who is enthroned on the clouds of heaven." [24] " The most remarkable thing about the painting," says Rojas, " is the motif, for the three Persons of the Trinity are represented by three identical persons. . . . The three . . . are in the act of crowning the Mother." [25]

An outstanding study of the view of Christ that prevailed from the beginning of the Spanish Conquest in Latin America is to be found in Dr. John A. Mackay's book *The Other Spanish Christ*. The main thesis of this book has not been successfully challenged in the quarter of a century since it was published, and its influence has been both wide and profound. It is that the Christ of Ramon Lull and of the great Spanish mystics such as Santa Teresa, San Juan de la Cruz, and others never reached the shores of Latin America. He was " the other Spanish Christ," the Christ whom Rojas was seeking earnestly and profundly when he said, " I feel that the Spirit of Christ . . . is something living and dynamic." [26]

Let us try to answer the question: Who was the Spanish Christ who went to Latin America?

According to Miguel de Unamuno, " The Spanish Christ was born in Tangiers." [27] " In other words," says Dr. Mackay, " he was a Christ who was not born in Bethlehem but in North Africa." [28] By that is meant that the popular faith of the African Moslem and the Spanish Catholic had become fused. This Christ has aesthetic and religious values, but is devoid of ethical demands.

Dr. Mackay describes a typical scene in Seville during Holy

Week. It is a scene of woe. " Scattered through the immense nave, across which the huge dark veil covering the high altar throws a gloomy shadow, women groan and lament the night long. . . . But after pealing bells have announced on the morrow that Christ is risen, the populace rises with him from its week of mourning . . . to attend the first bullfight of the season! The lack of an ethic in Spanish religion constitutes its problem, as it constitutes the problem of the religion transplanted in the New World." [29]

The Spanish Christ is a tragic victim. In Spain, as in Latin America, can be seen the bruised, livid, and blood-streaked images of Christ. One gains a deeper understanding of the contrast between the living, risen, eternal Christ and the dead Christ of Latin America by visiting the shrine on top of Montserrate Hill overlooking Bogotá, the capital of Colombia. The faithful come from far and near to worship at this shrine which contains an image of Christ in a glass case, a truly ghastly and depressing sight.

In many churches in Latin America the Virgin Mary is represented as the Queen of Heaven, full of life. In the cathedral of Buenos Aires, for example, one finds her high up above the main altar on a simulated throne, with pink cheeks and a crown on her head. On the side, among the statues of the saints, is the dead Christ on the cross, the suffering victim. Dr. Mackay describes the symbolism in these powerful words: " A Christ known in life as an infant, and in death as a corpse, over whose helpless childhood the Virgin Mother presides; a Christ who became man in the interests of eschatology, whose permanent reality resides in a magic wafer bestowing immortality; a Virgin Mother, who by not tasting death became the Queen of Life — that is the Christ and that the Virgin who came to America! He came as Lord of Death and of the life that is to be; she came as sovereign lady of the life that now is." [30]

Besides this worship of a dead Christ, there are other notable aspects of what Dr. Mackay calls " the Creole Christ." One of these is his lack of humanity. It is surprising how little is known of the life and teachings of Jesus in Latin America. The Nativity scene is familiar to many, as is the last week of Jesus' life, but the historical Jesus and his manhood are virtually unknown. There is a vague feeling that his was a blameless, sublime life, but the Jesus of the Gospels, and the risen Lord, are strangers to the Latin American people. This is one reason why Christ is not considered in the role of a mediator and why the intercession of Mary and of the saints is given such importance.

When Christ is not Lord, he becomes something other than the one we find in the New Testament story. In Latin America he is not supreme, power being shared with Mary and the saints. He has also become pluralistic, appearing as the Lord of Miracles, the Lord of the Holy Sepulcher, the Lord of Earthquakes, and many others, each image having its own special devotees and cult.

Without his sovereignty and Lordship, Christ's real significance is obscure and his power is diminished. Latin America has known a caricature of the Christ of the Gospels, and around his figure have grown up many superstitions and erroneous beliefs.

Because so many Latin Americans have never had a personal encounter with the living Christ, he has not occupied a rightful place in their lives. Christ as Redeemer and Savior is not known; the purity of his person and his message have been lost in the maze of ritual and the proliferation of deities.

VII

Religious Conditions in Latin America Today

A casual visitor to almost any South American country might be inclined to make a superficial judgment from the many outward evidences of religion that are to be seen, and conclude that he was in a solidly Christian country. He would be impressed by the number of magnificent churches, convents, and monasteries to be found in the cities and towns, some of which contain rare and valuable treasures and works of art. He would also be struck by the omnipresent priests in somber clerical garb, and friars in the habits of their various orders, to be seen in the larger communities. He would be awakened very early in the morning by the sound of church bells summoning the faithful to worship. If the visitor were to journey farther afield into the rural areas, he would notice the many wayside shrines and crosses that dot the countryside.

The term " Christian country " almost defies definition, for the criteria are difficult to establish. It would be truer to say that there is much religion in Latin America, religion being the outward manifestation, observance, or practice, as contrasted with the inward or spiritual experience, the changed life, ethical conduct, a commitment to high ideals, and a new kind of community, which are the hallmarks of the Christian faith.

It is our purpose in this chapter to discuss religious conditions in Latin America and, as we attempt to portray them, the reader will realize the importance of the historical events we have referred to, as well as the relevance of the sociological and psychological factors or patterns we have outlined.

We shall deal, first of all, with present-day religious conditions among the Indians who form a large section of the population in Mexico, Guatemala, Ecuador, Peru, and Bolivia.

AMONG THE INDIANS

In the previous chapter we have referred to the reaction of the Indian to Roman Catholicism when it was introduced into the New World by the Spaniards. What about his religious life today? What influence has Roman Catholicism exerted upon the millions of Indians to be found in the countries we have just mentioned? As has been stated: "Religion has not brought redemption to the Indian, human betterment and social uplift, or an abundant life. . . . He is continually kept impoverished or in debt because of the many *fiestas* or on account of the many demands made upon him." [1]

It is true that the sad condition of the Indian today is also attributable to a number of other factors, such as exploitation by the Spaniards, poverty and ignorance, with their concomitants, serfdom and landlessness, malnutrition and disease. By and large, it can be said that the Roman Catholic Church has done very little to uplift the Indian in three hundred years. (There have, of course, been honorable exceptions, notably the many self-sacrificing missionaries that Spain sent to the New World.) A Bolivian has this to say: "Unfortunately, with rare exceptions, the priest in the cantons is dissolute, avaricious, full of vices, and incapable of commanding respect; he receives money for Masses he never says, at least where and when he should, or he is content to say one Mass for many individuals when he has been paid for several; he loans money with interest and makes a fortune." [2]

On the whole the Indian today has very little comprehension of the meaning of Christianity. He is a Roman Catholic in name, but his Catholicism is a thin veneer over his pagan religion, or perhaps his religion can more accurately be described as a mixture of the two. After studying the Aymara Indians, an American anthropologist wrote: "Centuries of nominal Christianity have merely added another alien mythology to the body of Aymara beliefs. A brutally oppressed and cruelly exploited people, many of them have taken partially to the sadomasochistic symbols of the blood-dripping, thorn-crowned figure of Christ and the tragic-faced, all-merciful Mother, whom some of them identify with their own goddess. Although they all are accounted Christians, many of the Aymara hate the religion with the same vehemence as they hate its representatives." [3]

For the Andean Indian in Ecuador, Peru, and Bolivia, as well as for the Mexican and Guatemalan Indian, religion is primarily associated with the annual *fiesta* in honor of the patron saint of the village, when his image is carried through the streets in a procession. The local band accompanies the procession, and the participants sometimes dress in costume and wear masks. Several days are spent in dancing, drinking, and bullfighting, during which the Indian spends the savings of months; he may even end up in debt to the white man in the neighboring town. Thus religion is one of the main contributing causes of his poverty. His spiritual poverty often surpasses even his physical state of deprivation.

J. Merle Davis, who was a member of the commission appointed by the Committee on Cooperation in Latin America in 1943 to study the Andean Indian, described his condition as follows: " The problem of the Andean Indian is more than an economic-social problem. It is equally a spiritual and cultural problem. In the centuries of domination by the white man, the Indian has not only withdrawn physically, economically, and socially from his exploiters, retreating to physical elevations so great as to separate himself from modern life; he has also retreated into the inner recesses of his soul and has bolted and locked the door. Neither government, education, economic or social uplifters, or the church have yet discovered the key to that door. Behind it the Indian persists—impenetrable, indestructible, self-contained, unchanged and unchanging, preserving his ancient ideology, his gods, his values, his peculiar motivations, and his way of life." [4]

As the Indian in Latin America today understands very little of Roman Catholicism, he listens to Mass without comprehending it. Whether it be in Mexico, in Ecuador, or in Peru, one sees the Indian in abject submission, kneeling on the floor, overawed by the ritual that is in progress and impressed by the images and pictures, but there does not seem to be the slightest relationship between all that and the Indian's daily existence. In other words, there is a divorce between religion and life.

Back of the Indian's mind there seems to be the idea that was basic in his own pagan religion, that the gods or the saints are the ones who control his destiny and that they must be placated in some way. "They [the Ecuadorian Indians] ask a favor of a saint with the same faith and hope that they worship Imbabura, their mountain. They have faith also in witch doctors who, with equal ease, bring rain or prevent rain." [5]

Roman Catholicism with its pageantry, its ceremonies and *fiestas,* provides the Indian with an emotional release. The religious *fiestas,* with their pronounced social aspects such as dancing and drinking, enable the Indian to forget the drabness and the squalor of his daily life. They also give his submerged ego an opportunity to display itself before the group. Thus perhaps the most fundamental reason for the Indian's participation in the religious *fiesta* is a subconscious one. When he is sober, he is very much aware of the domination of the white man and of the exploitation his people have endured for centuries. When he gets drunk, he is no longer repressed or inhibited. "The white world recedes before them [the Indians] and makes way for the tide of passion. Drunk as gods, staggering with *chicha,* the Indians drink with a capacity and vigor unequaled in this world, drinking, dancing, drinking, till they fall unconscious in the equatorial sun. Yet the drinking and dancing is no orgy of dissipation. It is, rather, a summoning up of the violent energies of their life, an ecstasy, and an exaltation." [6]

It is for these values that the Indian esteems Roman Catholicism, rather than for any high moral principles which it might provide. "In those periods of crisis in life such as sickness, death, or drought, the Indian turns to his old religion for security. In time of danger to the individual as well as to the community, it is to the medicine man that the Indian turns." [7]

A strong element of fear is also found among the Indians. An illustration of this is the painting depicting hell, hanging in the Church of La Compañía in Quito, Ecuador. It is a large picture, and it shows all kinds of sinners being tortured, each in a different and " appropriate " way. The impure person has water running over his head and a vicious beast devouring his entrails; two women, one a vain woman, the other an adulteress, are also being preyed upon by animals; the cruel person is being strangled by a devil, and a homicide has knives thrust through his forehead. Each time the writer has visited this church he has found a group of Indians staring at this gruesome picture with their mouths open. It literally puts the fear of hell into them.

Christianity, far from being a redemptive force and an uplifting, transforming power in the lives of the Indians, has exercised a stultifying and even a degrading influence. It has deviated so widely from its pristine purity that Roman Catholic observers from the United States have been horrified by what they have seen and shocked by its sheer idolatry and superstition.

AMONG THE MESTIZOS IN RURAL AREAS

Rural people in any country are generally more simple and less sophisticated than urban dwellers; their range of knowledge is more limited, and yet they are often more religious. City folk tend to be more attracted to, and dominated by, the material interests of life. Country people in Latin America are no exception. In his sociological study of a village in Colombia called Saucío, Orlando Fals-Borda gives an excellent evaluation of the role of religion in the life of the people, and it can be considered typical of many other rural areas in Latin America.[8]

The patroness of the village is Our Lady of Health, and the priest and the mayor join forces in organizing the festivities in her honor in the month of October. A committee is appointed, with a leader, whose responsibility it is to collect money from each household for the decoration of the church, the outdoor altars, the musicians, and the fireworks. The *fiesta* lasts four days, and since many people come from neighboring villages, a great many patronize the tax-paying tents, where food and drinks are sold. Processions are held each day, and there is much dancing, singing, gambling and quarreling; the climax of the festivities is a bullfight, during which some of the drunkards usually get hurt.

Another *fiesta* is the one held in June in honor of Our Lady of Carmen, while at Christmas time everyone goes to midnight Mass and families have their private celebrations on Christmas Day. Instead of the Christmas tree, Latin Americans usually have a *crèche,* or nativity scene, with the baby Jesus, Mary, Joseph, and the shepherds.

The high point of the religious life of the village is Holy Week. This is no time for merrymaking or dancing, but for solemn faces, dark clothes, and an air of tragedy and gloom. After the three-hour sermon on Good Friday, the image of Jesus is taken down from the cross over the altar in the church and placed in the Holy Sepulcher; then there is an elaborate procession through the streets, in which images of the saints, the empty cross, and a statue of Mary are carried, while violins and flutes provide doleful music. Mourners pray, standing around the Holy Sepulcher all night. Early on Easter morning the image of Christ is taken from the sepulcher and once more nailed on the cross in the church.

The priest, besides presiding at religious festivals, performs duties such as baptisms, marriages, confirmations, and burials. Fees are charged for these services, and the money goes toward the upkeep of the church, as well as for the living expenses of the priest himself. Fees for burials are graded according to how elaborate the ceremony is; depending on such things as whether the priest leads the cortege around the main plaza or whether he goes directly to the cemetery.

The priest has the respect of most of the people, and they seek his advice on their problems. Fals-Borda believes that this respect for the priest and for the church is born partly out of fear. He says, " It is probably because of this fear and respect that the men are just as devout and churchgoing as the women." [9] The latter statement is not true all over Latin America, especially in the urban centers, where the majority of churchgoers are women.

The religious attitude of these rural people is one of resignation and complete trust. The individual has given up trying to understand the world in which he lives, if he ever tried seriously to do so; the church and *el cura* know more about these things, and so their instructions should be followed. This attitude produces a certain passivity in the individual, a negative stubbornness and fatalism. Even epidemics, it is believed, are sent from God, and therefore there is no use trying to check them. This fatalism resulted in resistance to the campaign to stamp out hoof-and-mouth disease in Saucío in 1951. " God is in charge of this world," the people said, " and his processes must not be interfered with." [10] The resistance was broken at a lower level, namely, the economic, when the farmers found they could not sell their cattle without a vaccination certificate.

Thus for the villagers the question in any given crisis or difficult situation is not, " What shall I do about it? " but, " What's the use? " This basic attitude accounts, in part at least, for the backwardness and lack of progress in many rural areas of Latin America; the people have surrendered their responsibilities and initiative to the church.

Fals-Borda says: " The Saucite [11] has a complete trust in God, the Virgin Mary, and the saints. Prayers directed to them are given a material shape in the form of burning candles. The lighting of a candle has deep emotional significance, literally meaning that while it burns in front of a sacred statue, painting, or picture, the candle is constantly reminding the saint of the things petitioned by the peasants." [12]

Here are devout, religious people; but religion seems to provide no joy, no spiritual buoyancy, and no victory. Perhaps it is because the Christ they worship is a dead Christ. " During Holy Week," says Fals-Borda, " it is not Christ's resurrection which interests the peasant — it is Christ's death. The death of Jesus and the descent from the cross, vividly re-enacted at the main altar of the church, bring forth a highly emotional response." [13] There seems to be no understanding of the redemptive role of Christ and the power of the risen Christ. In the church in Saucío he is a tragic victim, nailed to a cross with a crown on his head, a defeated, impotent Christ. In the words of Unamuno, quoted by Dr. Mackay: " Este Cristo de mi tierra es tierra " (This Christ of my native land is dust).[14]

For the villagers to take the image of Christ from his cross on Good Friday, place him in a sepulcher, and then return him to his cross on Easter Sunday is a highly emotional experience. It is a symbol of the common view of Christ, a dead Christ, a suffering victim, impotent and to be pitied.

" THE APOSTASY OF THE MASSES "

As we have stated already, it is a commonly held belief that the people of Latin America are solidly Roman Catholic. Writing in 1945, Richard Pattee, outstanding Roman Catholic layman who from 1938 to 1943 was Chief of the Division of Cultural Relations of the United States Department of State, said that the time had come to look the question straight in the face.[15] He came to the conclusion that Roman Catholics are only a minority in Latin America.

Pattee distinguishes two types of Roman Catholicism in Latin America. The first is the " sentimental brand largely practiced by pious older ladies." It is a Catholicism that can be seen in almost any small town or larger city in Latin America, at Mass on a weekday, at novenas or special devotions. Pattee calls it the " Catholicism of the black dress and mantilla." On Sundays these older women are joined by the younger ones, who are " dressed more to please the younger men than God."

Besides punctilious attendance at Mass, novenas, and special celebrations, there is a regular routine in the home which consists of drowsily reciting the rosary in some obscure corner. Pattee calls it a Catholicism without a spinal cord. It has very little, if any, effect on society and is unrelated to the problems of life.

The second type is that of an intellectual minority, small groups of ardent men who have captured some of the significance of Roman Catholicism as an ideology. Pattee says this is particularly true in Brazil. Roman Catholic thought has been revitalized in Chile and elsewhere by the outstanding French layman Jacques Maritain. According to Professor Gonzalo Baez Camargo, " Maritain has come to be within the Roman fold the most brilliant and outspoken defender of human rights, of freedom of conscience, of the conception of a nonpolitical church, and of a fraternal love between members of different creeds." [16]

Between these two types of Catholicism, the sentimental brand and the intellectual, ideological type, Pattee feels that there is a tremendous abyss; it is here that he finds the masses of Latin American people who, while nominally Roman Catholic and baptized into that faith, are not bound by any ties, sentimental or intellectual, of practice or profession. He asks the question whether they are lost to the Roman Catholic Church and, if so, why the church does not appeal to them. The problem, as he sees it, is how to win back the masses — the bulk of the population — that have drifted away.

One reason why the majority have drifted away, according to Pattee, is because the Roman Catholic Church has been too long tied to the conservative, landowning group, which is equivalent to saying the conversative political parties. The *latifundistas* have done much harm to the Roman Catholic Church by being closely related to it, not for any spiritual reasons, but because they believed the church stood for stability in the social order, which means the *status quo*. Some outstanding churchmen have been eager to break this pattern and to let the people see that the church is on the side of social justice. Typical of these are Archbishops Errásuriz and Caro. However, as Pattee points out, the overwhelming masses of the people are nominal Roman Catholics and are quite unaware of the social and economic teachings of the church.

There seems to be much confusion in the minds of the people as to the relationship the church should have to social and political questions, as can be seen in the example cited by Father Albert J.

Nevins.[17] He quoted an Argentine truck driver as saying that the priests should confine themselves to religious duties within their churches and not concern themselves with social and political matters. Such matters, he felt, had nothing to do with religion.

THE ROMAN CATHOLIC CHURCH AND RURAL PROBLEMS

The National Catholic Rural Life Conference of the United States, under the leadership of Monsignor L. G. Ligutti, has organized significant conferences on rural life in Latin America, the first of these being the one held in Manizales, Colombia, in 1953. The objectives of the Manizales Conference were: (1) to arouse interest in the spiritually and materially underprivileged rural people; (2) to promote the improvement of land tenure, conservation of land and water resources, and better agriculture; (3) to improve the spiritual, intellectual, and moral standards of rural homes and communities; and (4) to urge special spiritual care of rural families.

This conference was so successful in drawing attention to some of the most serious problems in rural Latin America that a second conference was held in Panama and a third in Santiago, Chile, which was attended by seven hundred delegates from many Latin American countries. One of the principal questions debated at this last conference was land tenure and, for the purposes of the discussion, former communists were brought over from Europe to warn the delegates of the disastrous consequences of the failure to solve this problem. Monsignor Ligutti said that land ownership was one of the most controversial issues, and a Latin American bishop stated that delegates should leave the conference determined to seek an immediate and fundamental solution of those problems of the land which prevent the farm worker from attaining that degree of human dignity and security to which he is entitled.

THE INTELLECTUALS AND UNIVERSITY STUDENTS

If, as Richard Pattee says, only a small minority of the intellectual group in Latin America have grasped the significance of Roman Catholicism, what about the majority? Generally speaking, Latin American culture is secular rather than Christian. The reason is that Christianity never captured the soul of the people because Roman Catholicism has been a religion rather than a profound faith, a set of practices, ceremonials, and observances, instead of a dynamic, compelling challenge to the human spirit. In a previous chapter we said that rationalism, Positivism, and Encylopedism produced a strong anticlerical and antireligious reaction in Latin America because the influence of the Reformation was not felt there as it was in the Anglo-Saxon world. Freethinkers are intellectuals who have found no spiritual home in Roman Catholicism, or have felt themselves emancipated from religious belief and dogma, being attracted by humanistic idealism with its political and social liberalism. The majority of the educated men and a minority of the educated women in Latin America are of this type; they are usually stanch defenders of civil rights and freedoms as well as constitutional government, and in socioeconomic affairs they are generally enlightened and progressive.

A well-known leader of the Radical Party in Argentina is typical of many in this group. For him, spiritual values are ideological or cultural values; he feels no need for the supernatural; he is a humanist with a passion for individual liberty and a respect for the dignity of human personality, but he has no use for religion.

In Uruguay one finds the reaction against Christianity symbolized by the fact that one important daily in Montevideo never capitalizes the word " God."

The freethinking, humanist type of intellectual has largely captured the universities in Latin America. Many of these universities were established by the church: San Marcos of Lima, San Carlos in Guatemala, those of the Dominican Republic, Mexico City, Santiago, and Bogotá. For centuries they were under the dogmatic control of a church that maintained a scholastic tradition and identified them with the cultural monopoly of colonialism. Following the achievement of political independence and the impact of European philosophical thought, these universities became what they are today, purely secular institutions. Latin America is not peculiar in this respect, as the same thing, more or less, has happened in the United States and Europe.

In Latin America the swing away from religious control was so complete that academic gowns were swept away too. In countries such as the Dominican Republic and Cuba, academic gowns are worn at graduation ceremonies, presumably through proximity to the United States, where it is seen that an academic gown has no religious significance.

In order to counteract the secular, Government-controlled universities, the Roman Catholic Church has been obliged to establish its own institutions of higher learning in order to maintain a Roman Catholic intellectual elite. If the Roman Catholic intellectuals are dogmatic, so are the freethinkers, many of whom were educated and nurtured in the Roman Church and acquired its cultural attitudes and mental habits. The Latin American freethinker has been called " a Catholic in reverse." Neither the Roman Catholic nor the freethinker regards Protestantism as being intellectually respectable. It must be admitted that the number of Protestant intellectuals is relatively small, although it is growing in Brazil, Mexico, and Argentina, and perhaps this is one of the reasons why the intelligentsia in Latin America considers the Protestant faith as having little intellectual appeal or basis. Another reason is that neither type of intellectual has the slightest understanding of what the Protestant faith is, nor is he aware of the noteworthy intellectual activity and profound scholarship among churchmen in Protestant countries such as Great Britain, Germany, and the United States.

Generally speaking, intellectuals and university students in Latin America are characterized by a religious indifference which has had some effect on the cultural, social, and political life of the Latin American countries. Perhaps nowhere else in the world is this phenomenon of religious indifference so pronounced. Here men have not wrestled with the great problems of truth, the soul, and life itself, and thus no great literature has been produced on the bearing of Christian truth on the great issues of today. There has been no great spiritual quest. In his book *The Invisible Christ,*

Rojas says: " In all Spanish America there is no serious study of these problems, no taste for them, no understanding of them. It is possible that in some countries, as in our own, for example, there has never been a real religious quest." [18]

The typical Latin American student has no faith in either Christianity or politics. His observations indicate to him that he can look to neither of them for the answers to the fundamental problems of life or of his deepest thinking. He is without a spiritual or ideological home, unless he becomes a positivist or a communist. Religion is for him synonymous with the Roman Catholic Church, and he rejects its medieval theology and superstitious practices. " To be Catholic," says Navarro Monzó, " signifies belonging to a determined group or orientation always conservative. . . . Purity of life, honesty in business, a spirit of charity, and an interest in community problems are of little or no importance. . . . The question is decided by the attitude which the man takes toward politics; if he votes in favor of the interests of the clergy and the monied classes, all is well." [19]

Julio Navarro Monzó believed that the " petrification of theology " of the Roman Catholic Church was largely responsible for widespread unbelief in Latin American countries, alongside " the lowest and grossest pagan superstition." [20]

THE MARYKNOLL FATHERS

One of the brightest spots in the picture of Roman Catholicism in Latin America is the work of the Maryknoll Fathers started in the 1940's and carried on by 120 priests and eight brothers in Chile, Bolivia, Peru, and Guatemala. Father Albert J. Nevins, Associate Editor of the Maryknoll magazine, writing in *The Sign,* says that although traditionally Latin America is Roman Catholic, in actual practice the people largely neglect their faith and the area can no longer be called a Catholic continent.[21] He states that it is the best mission continent in the world.

According to Father Nevins, the strength of the Roman Catholic Church in Latin America can be assessed as follows:

1. The church is strong and vital in Mexico, Costa Rica, Colombia, and Argentina;

2. The church is standing still in Guatemala, Nicaragua, El Salvador, Cuba, Chile, Venezuela, Peru, and Uruguay;

3. The church is dying in Bolivia, Paraguay, Brazil, Ecuador, Panama, Honduras, Dominican Republic, and Haiti.

Given this situation of the falling away from the church, the main purpose of the Maryknoll Missioners is to help to re-establish it; that is their missionary aim. " What is peculiar to missionary activity is that it aims to save souls by establishing the church." [22]

With deep sincerity and dedication, the Maryknoll Fathers devote themselves to this task, whether it be ministering to the Maya people of Guatemala whom they found largely pagan — or half pagan, half Christian — when they began work among them in 1943; or working high up on the Bolivian Altiplano, where many suffer hunger and cold and eke out an existence on appallingly low wages; or administering a high school and a seminary in Peru. The immediate objectives of the Maryknollers are: (1) to promote an intensive life of worship; (2) to help develop a vigorous apostolic spirit with the participation of the laity; (3) to create an active life of charity; and (4) to build up a strong Catholic home life.

In 1954, the Maryknoll Fathers held a Conference on Methods, from the report of which we have already quoted. This conference was remarkable for the forthright way in which those who attended it faced the realities of the Latin American situation, such as the fact that of the 154 million Roman Catholics in Latin America, the vast majority have no conception of what it means to be a Catholic; the stress on externals and accidentals rather than on essentials in the faith; the indifference of the people, and the fact that a Catholic in Latin America is more often than not a nominal one.[28] The findings include a section on Protestant techniques, with consideration of how they could be used to advantage. The techniques referred to are the participation of laymen in worship, the co-operation of the laity in religious and social action, and the emphasis on social welfare programs. In the discussion of these techniques, a bishop in Uganda was quoted as saying that while the Catholics seemed to practice the first commandment, to love the Lord their God, the Protestants have taken the lead with regard to the second, to love one's neighbor as oneself. The Protestants, he said, created neighborliness and went around prompting people to be kind to one another.

A study was also made of communist techniques. The report referred to a statement made by Canon Cardijn to the effect that communism is "the most dynamic and missionary movement of our times." In Latin America as elsewhere, it was pointed out, communism is more popular among the middle and upper classes, particularly the university students, than among the poor. It is believed that many are attracted to it because of some basic frustration in their lives, and because it seems to offer a concrete program which appeals to idealists. Father Considine, head of the Maryknoll Fathers, believes that one advantage the communists have over the Roman Catholics is that the former have no history of failure, while one of the problems of the church is trying to overcome the failures of two thousand years.

RELIGIOUS CONDITIONS IN BRAZIL

Although many religious conditions in Brazil are similar to those we find in Spanish-speaking Latin America, we are making special mention of them because there are important differences arising out of many diverse factors, such as the attitude of the Portuguese, the fact that colonization was slower, and the fact that there was no large settled Indian community such as in Mexico or Peru.

For thirty years after the Treaty of Tordesillas [24] in 1494, Portugal did virtually nothing to develop or colonize the vast area that had been assigned to it. Pedro Alvarez Cabral had claimed it formally in 1500, on one of his voyages of discovery, but Brazil was not the sort of rich prize men were looking for in that era of adventure. In 1530, the government of Portugal sent Martín Alfonso de Souza to establish a permanent colony. Originally he intended to sail to the River Plate, which he thought was east of the line of demarcation mentioned in the Treaty of Tordesillas. However, bad weather drove him back and he landed near what is now the port of Santos. There he established São Vicente, the first European settlement in Brazil. The system of setting up captaincies — which were large grants of land along the coast — was unsuccessful; São Vicente, however, flourished, as did also another settlement in Pernambuco.

The principal danger came from the Indians. The tribes found in Brazil were much less civilized than those encountered by the Spaniards in Mexico and Peru and the islands of the Caribbean. " They knew no metals, and their tools and weapons were made of polished stone or wood, their condition being more or less like that of prehistoric man." [25] The seminomadic tribes, mostly of the Tupi stock, were often at war with one another, and the Portuguese used this fact to their own advantage. At first some of the Indian chiefs accepted help from the Portuguese against their enemies, but due to the reckless cruelty of the Europeans and their use of slaves, the hostility of the Indians toward them was aroused.

The act of taking possession of the land was marked by the planting of a big wooden cross near the spot where the Portuguese landed, and by the celebration of Mass. " Brazil was born Christian," said Serafim Leiti. " It was born Christian above all through the faith that burned in the breast of the discoverers and their king." [26] Priests came with the first settlers, and it was not long before the Jesuits began their work among both colonists and Indians. The growth of the Roman Catholic Church in Brazil, in the early days as well as later, did not compare in vigor and extent to its development in other parts of Latin America. The outstanding Brazilian sociologist Gilberto Freyre says, " There was never in colonial Brazil a really powerful church or a strong clergy; nor were there domineering bishops, since each sugar planter, though a devout Catholic, was a sort of Philip II in regard to the church; he considered himself more powerful than the bishops or abbots." [27]

The Jesuits were the most important religious order in Brazil during the colonial period, until they were expelled in 1759. Their first mission arrived in 1549, just seven years after the Society of Jesus was formed in Europe. An integral part of the Counter Reformation movement, the Jesuits were aggressive and vigorous; conditions in Brazil represented a great challenge to their energies, and they soon became one of the chief civilizing and unifying forces in the land.

The outstanding figures in the early days were Father Manuel de Nobrega, who went to Brazil in 1549 as director of the first group of Jesuits, and Father José de Anchieta, who arrived in 1553. Anchieta labored there for forty-seven years, and he has a prominent place among the world's great Christian missionaries. He was a scholar and a tireless worker; his fame as a teacher, preacher, and healer spread far and wide. He learned the Tupi language and founded the first classical school in America, gathering twenty pupils in a little mud hut. It was not long before the Jesuits began to develop an educational system for the children of the colonists and the Indians.

At the same time, the plantation system grew up, and with it Negro slavery on a large scale. Most of the time the Jesuits were in conflict with both. However, Roman Catholic beliefs and practices did not dominate entirely. As a large number of African slaves were brought to Brazil, it was inevitable that African beliefs, rites, and superstitions should permeate the cultural life of that country. Azevedo says that the Christian life was so contaminated with " Afro-Indian impurities," and there was so much immorality and dissoluteness of custom, that the white race was threatened with extinction in the seventeenth and eighteenth centuries.

Although a fusion has taken place with Catholicism, the *Candomblé,* or Afro-Brazilian fetish cult, is still a vigorous institution, particularly in the Salvador area in the state of Baía, where there are probably two hundred *seitas,* or worship centers. According to

Charles A. Gauld, student of religious conditions in Brazil, "Brazilian black magic of syncretic Catholic-Afro-Brazilian type has been rapidly spreading, to the distress of Catholic priests and Protestant pastors." [28]

In the large cities, spiritualist centers are numerous, there being seven thousand incorporated spiritualist societies and fifteen thousand nonincorporated in the whole country. In São Paulo, the Esoteric Circle of Communion of Thought has over fifty thousand members. It is estimated that there are ten million spiritualist members in Brazil.

RESURGENCE OF ROMAN CATHOLICISM

Two facts have given great concern to leaders of the Roman Catholic Church, whether it be in Rome, the United States, or Latin America itself; these are, the decline and loss of power and prestige of the church in Latin America and the growing strength of the Evangelical movement. [29]

These two facts account largely for the attempts to revive Roman Catholicism in various aspects and emphases. In the first place, there is a new emphasis on aesthetic values, always an integral factor in Latin religious cultures. There is a resurgence of the splendor and pageantry as well as the worship of relics and images. Replicas of the famous image of Our Lady of Fatima, and the Holy Cross of Jerusalem, which is reputed to contain a splinter of the actual cross of Calvary, have toured several countries.

The best example of religious pageantry was the International Eucharistic Congress held in Rio de Janeiro in July, 1955. A large area had been reclaimed from the bay so that this huge congress could be held in the open air. Its main purpose was a mass affirmation of faith in the Eucharist, the bodily presence of Christ in the Blessed Sacrament. At a given signal, a high-ranking prelate unrolled a Vatican parchment and read a papal bull, while a hundred torch-lighted vessels in Guanabara Bay escorted the Blessed Sacrament to the altar; guns were fired and varicolored searchlights played impressively on the surrounding hills.

Another aspect of Roman Catholic revival is the new interest in the Bible. Departing from the traditional policy of the church, two new Spanish translations of the Scriptures which have appeared in recent years were made directly from the Hebrew and Greek originals. Another commendable innovation is the reading of the Scriptures in the language of the country, while Mass is being said.

The Roman Catholic Church also continues to use political power as a means of increasing its own strength as an ecclesiastical system and becoming a greater force in society. The outstanding examples are Colombia and Mexico.

During the Civil War which lasted from 1949 until 1953 in Colombia, and in the political turmoil of succeeding years, the Roman Catholic Church not only supported dictatorships, but sought by every means to eradicate the Protestant minority. Seldom has the persecution of a religious minority in modern times assumed such proportions or been carried on in such a relentless way. Fanatical elements took advantage of what appeared to be the official attitude of the Government and the church toward Protestants, and the persecution took the form of destroying or damaging church properties, killing or injuring individuals, closing churches and schools, imprisoning pastors and members of churches, and waging a systematic campaign of defamation in the press and over the radio.[30] Later, when the dictator Rojas Pinilla tried to form a third party based on labor, as Perón did in Argentina, and when he was fast losing popularity in the nation, the hierarchy turned against him and hastened his fall in May, 1957. The church, which at one time had supported the dictator, then claimed credit for having ousted him.

In Mexico, much has written in recent years to show how the Roman Catholic Church is trying to regain the power and wealth it lost in the social revolution that began in 1910. "The history of Mexico, since the Conquest, has been upset by the constant intervention of the Catholic clergy. In our country the clergy has always been belligerent in economic, social, and political affairs."[31] Evidently Mexican writers are aware of the intensification of this intervention on the part of the hierarchy in an attempt to reassert its hegemony.

As part of the political offensive, there has also been an upsurge in Mariolatry in some countries. " The Marian cult, namely, the exaltation of the Virgin Mary, is not a simple homage to the mother of Christ. It is a political theory, as well as an economic one. In fomenting the cult of Mary and in choosing the Virgin of Guadalupe as an emblem of the Christian social order in Latin America, that is to say, in the struggle for the Kingdom of the Virgin of Guadalupe, which is nothing but the predominance of the church over the state, the church exploits the religious sentiments of the Latin American people, especially the hopeless Indian masses and the women." [32]

Another aspect of the attempt to revitalize Roman Catholicism is the campaign in some countries against prostitution, pornographic literature, excessive drinking, and gambling. This is to be welcomed, particularly in view of the wide separation between religious belief and ethical conduct or practice that has always existed.

It is undoubtedly true that Protestant Christianity has had a beneficial effect on Roman Catholic practice. It was reported to the writer that in a certain Latin American country a Roman Catholic bishop once said he would like to see a Protestant missionary or pastor in every parish in his diocese.

PROTESTANTISM

Protestantism in Latin America has grown steadily from small beginnings in the nineteenth century, but the most rapid growth has been since World War I. In 1916 there were less than 200,000 Protestants in all Latin America, and today there are five million. This growth has been largely in Brazil, Mexico, Chile, Argentina, Puerto Rico, Guatemala, Peru, and Colombia.

The Protestant faith has made its appeal mostly to the middle and lower classes; very little effective work has been done among either the industrial workers or the intellectual class.

One of the greatest contributions of Protestant missions has been in the field of education. Through the schools that have been established, the Evangelical people have been able to educate their children, and the influence of the educational work of several decades is now being felt. The children of the former poorer classes have become the professional men, the doctors, lawyers, teachers, businessmen, and government employees of today. It has been said that the Evangelical churches of Latin America are producing their own elite.

Thus the strength of Protestantism becomes at the same time a weakness. While it is a fact that a middle class is the backbone of a democratic society, it is also true that to make a total impact on society, the gospel must spread not only along one stratum of society but through all, reaching especially the working classes and the intellectuals. The Evangelical church needs many more capable leaders, as well as a more diversified constituency.

The Evangelical churches have had to face the problem of their foreign origin. The gospel was brought by North American and European missionaries, and it was inevitable that they should carry their message in cultural molds and patterns that were different from those of Latin America. The Evangelical churches have had to depend largely on Anglo-Saxon literature and hymnology, translated into Spanish, Portuguese, and the Indian languages, and architectural forms have mostly had to be imported. There is an increasing tendency, however, to create indigenous music, drama, and literature, and to develop a Latin American architecture in church construction, but the process has only just begun.

Because of its rapid development in recent decades, Protestantism suffers from many of the growing pains associated with a new movement, such as insufficient and inadequately trained leadership, an overemphasis on the pietistic and individual aspects of Christianity, to the neglect of the whole gospel and the role of the church in the world, a fissiparous tendency, and the unwillingness of some groups to co-operate with others. Undoubtedly some of these weaknesses will diminish as young, dynamic leadership develops and takes its place in the church councils.

In addition to the factors we have mentioned, there is a lack of a real concept of what the Christian church is. This is seen quite markedly in some of the fast-growing independent groups; or what we might call the nonhistoric Protestant groups.

In spite of the many problems and difficulties they are faced with, the Protestant or Evangelical churches have taken root in the soil of Latin America and in the hearts and minds of its people. A new day is dawning.

VIII

Religion
and Dynamic Faith

We have now arrived at a point where we must examine more closely the difference between religion and faith. This brings us to the heart of the main thesis of this book. It is no accident that the great Reformers such as Luther and Calvin, as well as a foremost Protestant theologian such as Karl Barth, should find Paul's epistle to the Romans so basic to their theological position and thinking.

As a result of reading the epistle to the Romans, Luther distinguished between the law and the gospel. Melanchthon said that Luther refuted the error which then reigned in the schools and assemblies, which taught that men merit remission of sins by their own works and that men are justified with God by discipline, as the Pharisees had taught. The importance to Luther of the difference between religion and Christian faith cannot be overestimated. " The turning point in Luther's theology," says Leonard D. Agate, " was reached when he lectured on the epistle to the Romans." [1]

RELIGION AS LAW RIGHTEOUSNESS

Martin Luther said that the author of religion is the devil. Karl Barth has this to say: " Religion is the working capital of sin." [2] " Religion is not a thing to be desired or extolled; it is a misfortune which takes fatal hold upon some men. . . . Conflict and distress, sin and death, the devil and hell, make up the reality of religion. So far from releasing men from guilt and destiny, it brings men under their sway. . . . Religion possesses no solution to the problem of life; rather, it makes of the problem a wholly insoluble enigma." [3]

All these are rather strong statements on the subject of religion, and may come as a surprise to those who have always been accustomed to thinking that to be religious was a state of mind or spirit highly to be desired, or that religion is something that the Christian church " promotes." " The revelation in Christ," says Hendrik Kraemer, " stands apart from all religions — not as a unique individual case of a common species, but as a different genus. It is *sui generis*." [4] Kraemer goes farther and says that the Christian revelation is the crisis of all religions. Christian faith, which means that God revealed himself in Christ, is not a special kind of religion; it does not fit into the generally accepted concept of the term.

Jesus Christ did not come into the world to give us a religion; as a matter of fact, he reserved his most scathing denunciations for the religious people of his day. It was mainly because he opposed, and became a serious threat to, the Jewish ecclesiastical leaders that they conspired to have him put to death.

What, then, was Jesus concerned with in human life and what did he believe was the secret of an abundant life? John answers that question when he says: " In him was life; and the life was the light of men " (John 1:4). Jesus himself said that he had come that men might have abundant life. Thus faith in Christ as the revelation of God himself, and as a living eternal reality, is the answer, rather than religious observances and practices. What is needed today, what Latin America needs, is not more religion, but more faith and truly abundant life. To understand the difference between religion and Christian faith is to comprehend the difference between men and God. To read and understand Paul's writings is to realize that this was the main theme of his message to the early churches and to the Christians of his time and of all time. Before King Agrippa he says, " That after the most straitest sect of our religion I lived a Pharisee. And now I stand and am judged for the hope of the promise made of God unto our fathers " (Acts 26:5-6).

Before his conversion Paul was a religious man: "For ye have heard of my conversation in time past in the Jews' religion" (Gal. 1:13). After his conversion Paul was a man of faith, and the word "faith" appears over and over again in his letters to the newly formed Christian churches. "And the life which I now live in the flesh I live by the faith of the Son of God" (Gal. 2:20). "For by grace are ye saved through faith" (Eph. 2:8). Paul's writings also contain many references to what is called "law righteousness": "not having mine own righteousness, which is of the law, but that which is through the faith of Christ, the righteousness of which is of God by faith" (Phil. 3:19). Before his conversion he strove after his own righteousness. He liked to think that he lived up to the stern and rigid standards of morality and good citizenship and that he was meticulous in the performance of his religious duties. After his conversion his gaze turned from his own righteousness to that of Christ, which he apprehended by faith.

The religion of many people in the world today is similar in nature, consisting of attempts at good works and pride in good character. It is a religion based on law, duty, and merit, and the sense of justification that actions in accordance with these bring. The motivation is one of self-approval or of feeling justified in one's own eyes. Paul terms it "justification by works," and after his dramatic encounter with Christ on the road to Damascus, he came to see that this kind of justification is self-centered rather than God-centered; in other words, it is an expression of man's egoism.

In the New Testament, the sense of the word "justification" is the opposite of self-justification, and fundamentally involves a concept of the real nature of God and a realization of man's own nature, as well as a right relationship between God and man. Writing out of his own profound experience, Paul came to see that religion that meant ritual, religious institutions, outward observances and ceremonies was not the answer to man's basic problem, namely, his own sinful nature and his relationship to God. The only valid use of the term "Christian religion" is when a person has come to know God through Christ and experienced forgiveness through his saving grace, and continually feels the need to cultivate the presence of God through devotions or worship. Religion as devotions, or worship, focuses the attention on God, his greatness, his love, and his mercy, rather than on one's own goodness, actions, or piety. The word " worship " comes from two old Anglo-Saxon words which put together mean " worthship "; thus " worship " is a concentration on the " worthship " or greatness of God.

" Protestantism," says Harnack, " is a rediscovery of religion as faith, as a relation between person and person, higher, therefore, than all reason, and living not upon commands and codes, but in the power of God, and apprehending in Jesus Christ the Lord of Heaven and Earth as Father." [5]

Karl Barth says that the reality of religion lies in the utter questionableness of man's ego, a disgust of men at themselves, in a realization of their inability to do what they should do. Paul expressed it thus: " For I know that in me (that is, in my flesh) dwelleth no good thing: for to will is present with me; but how to perform that which is good I find not. For the good that I would, I do not: but the evil which I would not, that I do " (Rom. 7:18-19). This dualism of the law of the mind or of the spirit and the law of sin " which is in my members " is what concerns Paul, for that is where the conflict is; and he proclaims: " O wretched man that I am! who shall deliver me from the body of this death? I thank God through Jesus Christ our Lord " (Rom. 7:24-25).

It is at this point that we find the profound meaning of the incarnation, the life and the death of Christ. God revealed himself fully and supremely in Jesus Christ and sought to redeem man, to blot out the remembrance of his sin, and to remove his guilt for all time by a saving faith in the finished work of Christ on the cross.

Religion that does not bring man to a recognition of his own complete unworthiness and utter dependence on the mercy of God is sterile. Karl Barth puts it this way: " Religion spells disruption, discord, and the absence of peace." [6]

"Do Ut Des" — A Bargaining with God

There is a widespread belief in Latin America that man can earn the favor of God " by doing something " or performing some act; that he can achieve peace of mind and reconciliation with God; in a word, that God will accept him and he will be justified, i.e., considered good, if he does this or that. Religion in Latin America is largely of the *do ut des* type (the phrase *do ut des* means: " I give in order that thou mayest give "). In essence this form of religion is a kind of bargaining with God and, as we have seen, it was fundamental in the pre-Columbian religions. In popular Catholicism in Latin America, the system of penances, payment for Masses and prayers and indulgences, is nothing but a bargaining with God for special favors and privileges.

In his sociological study of a village in Colombia, Fals-Borda found that " the main reasons for the peasants' regular attendance at church seem to be these: the bargaining for favors from the saints, the avoidance of the accumulation of penalties when confession time comes, and the fear of incurring God's displeasure and going to hell." [7] Thus the system of bargaining is extended to the saints.

It is often the case in Latin America that unmarried women keep a statue of Saint Anthony in some corner of the house, or in a niche, and light candles to him and pray to him for a husband. When he fails to provide suitors, Saint Anthony may be stood on his head or turned to the wall in disgust. There is a story of one case where prayers to Saint Anthony resulted in the appearance on the scene of a husband for the young lady. Repeated supplications had failed, and in anger and disappointment, she took the statue and threw it out of the window. The image happened to hit a young man who was walking along the street, and he came to the house in high dudgeon to demand an explanation. The acquaintance thus established with the thrower of the image blossomed into romance and marriage!

Religion is telling God what *we* have done, or will do, so that he will give us what we want. Faith begins when we listen to what God is telling us; and what he tells us is the good news that by faith in Christ as Savior we may experience the forgiveness of sins and have newness of life.

PROTESTANTISM

In our discussion of religion and faith in Latin America, we must now ask what is the meaning of the word "Protestant" and what Protestantism is. The word "Protestant" was originally used in an affirmative sense at the time the declaration was made by the Lutheran princes in 1529; their "protestation" was an affirmation of the liberty of reforming diets.[8] The word "protest" was also used affirmatively in Shakespeare's time. In one of his plays, he says: "I have a wife whom I protest I love," and there was nothing negative about that statement. A modern dictionary such as Webster's defines the verb "to protest" as follows: (1) to assert; affirm; aver; (2) to make a protest against; as, to protest a witness. The negative meaning or use is even today secondary. The same dictionary gives the derivation of the word from the Latin *protestari* (from *pro* + *testari*) meaning, "to be a witness." This etymology of the word gives vital and rich meaning to the term "Protestant"; to be a Protestant means to be a witness, or to testify for one's faith.

The heart of the Protestant movement is the witness that men and women bear to the power of Jesus Christ to transform and renew life from within, speaking out of firsthand knowledge, as a witness must do. "I know whom I have believed," said Paul. As Kant, the Protestant philosopher, affirmed, knowledge of God can only be based on personal experience of him and not on rational proof, as Thomas Aquinas maintained. Protestants must be witnesses for Christ and his redemptive power.

Religion always tends in time to become institutionalized; its inspiration congeals or evaporates. It mixes with earlier forms of belief and traditional modes of worship and embraces even primitive superstitions. Religion, in the sense in which we have used it, involves a priesthood, and sooner or later it is drawn into secular interests and political machinations. It is the nature of

Protestantism to check the tendency toward corruption and rigidity which is found in organized religion. " Essentially Protestantism is not a theological system; it is a spirit — the spirit of reverent and courageous challenge of whatever stands in the way of truth." [9]

Protestantism stands for ethical principles as over against ceremonial rules. The prophets of the Old Testament were Protestants in their time; they preached justice, mercy, and truth; they thundered against sacrifice, ceremony, and ritual, practices that not only were devoid of ethical content but had become heavy burdens on the people. Jesus himself was in the same prophetic succession, and his utterances were characterized by a revolt against the religious practices of his day. " Thou blind Pharisee, cleanse first that which is within the cup and platter, that the outside of them may be clean also " (Matt. 23:26). The process of renovation was from within outward. As W. R. Inge, former dean of St. Paul's Cathedral, London, and a prominent Anglican in his day, put it, " Christ taught a very radical Protestantism." [10] While the earlier prophets sought moral and social reform, Jesus made a revolution. " He abolished at a stroke the whole principle of religious hierarchies." [11]

Protestantism also was a return to primitive Christianity, and only as it seeks to renew itself constantly at the original source of truth, the New Testament, is it true to itself and to the Lord it seeks to glorify. The New Testament, as the Protestant Reformers discovered, was the New Covenant. Let Dean Inge speak to this: " Christ abolished all barriers of race, color, sex, and church by ignoring them. The exclusiveness of the Jewish church was utterly abolished. No intermediaries are needed between God and man. There is an end of all material sacrifices; the only acceptable sacrifice under the New Covenant is the consecration of ourselves. The law of love embraces all that need be retained of the old legislation. He founds no new religion, in the ordinary sense of the word; he institutes no creed, no priests, no sacred writings." [12]

The authority for the affirmation that Christ abolished the

priesthood, except in the sense that all believers are priests, is none other than Paul. " Having therefore, brethren, boldness to enter into the holiest by the blood of Jesus, by a new and living way, which he hath consecrated for us, through the veil, that is to say, his flesh " (Heb. 10:19-20). It is significant, therefore, that with the coming of Christ the New Testament no longer recognizes the validity of the priesthood as it is found in the Old Testament, nor any type that is bound up with a religious hierarchy.

The true Christian church which grew out of New Testament times knows no priestly caste, simply because the emphasis is on faith, rather than on religion; it is faith in the finished work of Jesus Christ on the cross as the Savior of mankind, a faith in God as revealed in the Person of Jesus Christ; it is faith that " God was in Christ, reconciling the world unto himself " (II Cor. 5:19).

FOUR PILLARS OF PROTESTANTISM

The four pillars of Protestantism have been described as: the priesthood of all believers, justification by faith, the right of private judgment, and the authority of the Word of God as revealed in the Bible.[18] We shall deal with these briefly, in order to demonstrate their relevancy in Latin America, as well as their basic importance in the development of the Protestant movement.

The priesthood of all believers is fundamental in Protestant faith and practice. Inasmuch as Christ opened up a new and living way to God through his own Person, it is the privilege of every believer to have direct communion with God, without going through a priest as intermediary. This does not mean that a Protestant must never consult his pastor, but when he does it is with the understanding that both are equal before God and one does not have more access to him than the other. The priesthood of all believers also means that a Christian mediates God in Christ to his fellow men. Calvin said that " all of God's people are his clergy." That is to say, there is no difference between clergy and laity, so far as prerogatives are concerned.

This doctrine of the priesthood of all believers " gives to the ordinary man a dignity and understanding which are matched in no other teaching. It places a new value on the common life and labor as it rejects the division between religious life and the secular life." [14] The doctrine also means that a man is accountable to God for his actions in the intimacy of his own soul; this develops moral character. It is also the foundation of democracy.

The second pillar is the doctrine of justification by faith. The authority for this is the phrase from Paul's writings: " The just shall live by faith " (Rom. 1:17). Salvation does not come by any outward observance or performance or by belonging to any church; it does not depend on any system of bargaining that a priest may have with God on another man's behalf. As we have already seen in our discussion of religion and faith, this was a system of bondage from which Paul sought deliverance, and the release or liberation came when he experienced justification through faith in Christ, which all his good works could not buy.

Thus it is not through our own merit, or even through the church, that we enter into a right relationship with God, which alone can bring peace; but, as the Reformers discovered and then proclaimed, through an act of faith or trust in God through Christ. Here we come to the heart of the Christian faith as contrasted with religion, at least religion based on a priesthood and an ecclesiastical system. According to the Roman Catholic religion, if a person surrenders his will to the church and obeys its commandments, he will be acceptable to God. A papal encyclical said: " The Roman Catholic Church is essentially an unequal society, a society composed of two categories of persons: pastors and the flock. . . . With the pastors alone resides the necessary right and authority to guide and direct all the members toward the goals of society. As for the multitude, it has no other right than that of allowing itself to be led and as a docile flock to follow its shepherds."

The gospel or good news is that God's love was revealed in the death of his Son on the cross and that through his death God was reconciling the world unto himself. " The next day John seeth Jesus coming unto him, and saith, Behold the Lamb of God, which taketh away the sin of the world! " (John 1:29).

Man does not have to perform any rite, or to *do* anything in order to rid himself of guilt; all that is required of him is to accept God's forgiveness by faith in Christ. He can be justified only through the merits of Christ himself and not through his own works or acts. That is the gospel as it is found in the New Testament; it is the Protestant faith.

The third pillar of Protestantism is the right of private judgment. Protestantism respects freedom of conscience; Roman Catholicism is a religion of authority. No institution, not even the church, has the right to tell a person what to believe in the Bible and what books to read or not to read. Every Christian has the right to follow the dictates of his own conscience with the guidance of the Holy Spirit. Christian congregations have the right to determine who shall be their church officers and who shall be their pastor; in other words, the right of private judgment extends to the organization of the church which is the body of believers. The right of private judgment has had a profound influence on the establishment of human rights and the development of free democratic societies and institutions.

The fourth pillar is the authority of the Word of God. The question of authority in matters of the spirit has always been an important one. The Roman Catholic Church teaches that authority resides in the church and in its head, the pope, and in tradition. Protestants believe in the authority of the Bible as the Word of God, and this faith has played an important part in the Reformation and the subsequent development of the church.

In Latin America the Bible was virtually unknown until the advent of Protestantism. One of the precursors of the Protestant movement in the early nineteenth century was James Thomson, and his work in various South American countries was a symbol of two important phases of Protestantism, the dissemination of the Bible among the people and education. Thomson was a Bible Society agent and a schoolteacher. Wherever Protestant missionaries have gone they have stood for the central place of the Bible in Christian life and for education by means of the establishment of schools.

Historically, a great impetus was given to education at the time of the Reformation by making the Bible available to the common people in their own language, and it is no accident that Scotland has so long been known for its excellent school system. The early Reformers saw to it that a school was built near each church, for if the Bible as the Word of God was now available to the people, then they must be taught to read it.

PROTESTANTISM, FREEDOM, AND DEMOCRACY

The four pillars of Protestantism, namely, the priesthood of all believers, justification by faith, the right of private interpretation, and the authority of the Word of God, are also of fundamental importance in the development of a free democratic society. "Democracy and Christianity," says Navarro Monzó, "are twin brothers, born of the same blood which was shed twenty centuries ago on a cross." [15] Christianity emphasizes such virtues as a basic respect for moral law, individual human rights and freedoms, and brotherhood, without which democracy cannot flourish.

We have seen in a previous chapter how the Protestant principle of the will of the people was enshrined in the constitutions of the Latin American countries. It is also true to say that they grant religious freedom in one form or another. We have also seen that these principles exist as great ideals of the people, but, with few exceptions, the forces of history have militated against their being anything but ideals. Although the pattern varies from country to country, it can be said that the history of Latin America for the past one hundred and fifty years has been a struggle for freedom and democracy as over against authoritarianism and clericalism. The struggle for religious freedom still continues.

In his book *Cuestiones Colombianas,* Alfonso López Michelsen observes that the right to be wrong springs from the right of private judgment, and it is a concession which the Protestant makes with ease. "The Catholic," he says, "does not understand this, because instinctively he tries to make a dogma out of his political convictions, and he does not admit the existence of certain matters over which there might be discussion and agreement." [16] Dr. López makes the interesting comment that in Roman Catholic countries the state is conceived as paternalistic, good and kind, in the same way as God is thought of. People expect favors from the government just as they expect favors as well as miracles from God.

It is strange how long it takes for the concept of religious freedom to come to fruition. In Protestant countries it was not achieved without struggle and a long process of evolution; the settlers in New England who had left the Old World because they were not free to worship God according to their conscience, sometimes denied the same right to others and became intolerant of divergent religious beliefs.

The Roman Catholic view of religious freedom has been succinctly expressed by Father Francis J. Connell in his booklet *Freedom of Worship, the Catholic Position.* The gist of this can be stated as follows: the Catholic Church is the only organization authorized by God to teach religious truth, and thus no one has a genuine right to profess any but the Catholic religion. The mere fact that a person believes a certain religion to be true does not give him the right to accept it or practice it in an unrestricted form. This is called " doctrinal intolerance." However, there is another principle known as " personal tolerance," which means that Catholics must presume that those who differ from them in religious belief are sincere, unless the opposite is evident, and supernatural love must embrace all regardless of their religious belief or unbelief. In Catholic countries the civil rulers are justified in restricting, or even preventing, denominational activities that are contrary or hostile to the Catholic religion. " This does not mean that they may punish or persecute those who do not accept the Catholic faith." [17] However, even in Catholic countries circumstances may make it advisable for the government to grant non-Catholics the same religious freedom and the same civil rights that Catholics enjoy, but only so long as it is recognized that only the Catholic religion has a God-given right to exist.

In Latin America, according to the Roman Catholic hierarchy, freedom of religion means freedom for the one true religion, namely, the Roman Catholic. Moreover, the church firmly believes that that religion should be protected and favored by the state. Wherever possible, it maintains, there should be a concordat with the Vatican, such as exists in Colombia.

The Protestant point of view regarding religious freedom is summed up in the paragraph contained in the Universal Declaration of Human Rights of the United Nations (1943), as follows: "Everyone has the right to freedom of thought, conscience, and religion; this right includes freedom to change his religion or belief, and freedom either alone or in community with others and in public or private, to manifest his religion or belief in teaching, practice, worship, and observance."

There is another fundamental difference between the Roman Catholic and Protestant viewpoints: the former is based on the belief that governments may grant religious freedom, whereas the Protestant position is that religious freedom and freedom of conscience are a God-given right.

A Dynamic Faith

Earlier in this chapter we touched very briefly on the profound theological problems of religion and faith. A longer discussion of them would be out of place except in a treatise on theology. However, we have felt it necessary to raise the issue because it is inescapable in our discussion of the fundamental problem in Latin America, as anywhere else — that of man in his relationship to God. It is peculiarly relevant to the issues in Latin America, since in no other great area of the world has religion been so omnipresent and nowhere else has it failed so conspicuously to achieve what true religion should accomplish.

We must now ask whether it is not possible for the experience we call faith to be unfruitful and barren also. The answer to that question is that "even so faith, if it hath not works, is dead" (James 2:17). The advocates of the doctrine of salvation by works sometimes try to make a case against the doctrine of salvation by faith by alleging that faith alone is useless. There is validity to this point of view and, as we have just pointed out, it has Biblical support. However, genuine faith cannot be barren and fruitless, for if it produces no fruit it is not genuine.

In his excellent study of the relevance of Paul's epistle to the Ephesians to the times in which we live, Dr. John A. Mackay traces the nature and the unfolding of God's order. In this drama there is theology, mysticism, liturgy, poetry, and Christian ecclesiology. In his final chapter, Dr. Mackay arrives at this conclusion: "But the divine purpose cannot be fulfilled, nor can Christians fulfill their destiny, save in concrete action." [18]

Jesus said, "Follow me" — i.e., be my disciples and learn of me — but he also told the parable of the good Samaritan and ended by saying, "Go, and do thou likewise." Finally he said, "Go ye therefore, and teach all nations" (Matt. 28:19).

True Christian faith is dynamic; it has compelling force and direction. It led and inspired a Wilberforce to fight a political battle against slavery in the British Empire; it impelled a Schweitzer to give secondary place to philosophy, music, and even theology, in order to give himself to a life of devotion to unfortunate, underprivileged human beings and carry on a struggle against some of the evils of our time; it enabled a Francis of Assisi to give up the comfortable life of a wealthy young man to serve the poor; and it moved a Father Damian to sacrifice his life in dedication to lepers.

"Faith in the New Testament," says Tillich, "is the state of being grasped by the divine Spirit." [19] Faith, used in this sense, is the Holy Spirit indwelling the human mind with compelling power. Dr. Mackay expressed it thus: "God requires that the citizens of his Kingdom should act, should walk, should fight, should ever move toward the frontiers where the crucial issues are." [20] "Put on the whole armor of God," said Paul in his letter to the Ephesians (Eph. 6:11).

This is the call that comes to all Christians today, as it comes to the Evangelicals in Latin America. It is a call to action, indeed to participation in the struggle against evil in all its forms. There may be some in the churches who are content with the ecstatic mystical experience of individual salvation and have forgotten Paul's clarion call to action in the struggle against principalities and powers, spiritual wickedness, and — we might add — social evils and injustice.

Latin America today needs the whole gospel. It needs men and women of faith, not just faith for their own satisfaction and peace of mind, but a dynamic, compelling faith. Such men and women will be crusaders in the war against evils and injustices in the society in which they live. They will see that the church of which they are a part does not withdraw from the world into a comfortable, mystical round of spiritual exercises unrelated to the world of sin and darkness.

THE POWER OF HIS RESURRECTION

There are many Latin Americans with only a nominal relationship to any Christian church; they can be charming people, with a wide knowledge of the world in general and high ideals. In more intimate conversation with liberal, cultured men, one often finds they have a special regard or respect for Jesus of Nazareth as a moral example. They may even believe there is some relationship between the ideals and teachings of Christ and the freedom and democracy which they would like to see their country enjoy. What such men lack is power, not ideals. Jesus never said, " Come unto me and I will give you a set of ideals." He did say, " Ye shall receive power." Without this, modern man is immobilized.

The Evangelical faith is not just the faith of Christmas, or of Good Friday, but of Easter. What did the preaching of the early church point to? It was not the birth of Jesus, nor his death, but his resurrection. That was the authenticating event by which God spoke decisively and powerfully to men. In the resurrection faith God offers salvation and power to men, not because they merit it through any moral achievement of their own, but because of his active, seeking, reconciling love. God took the initiative in revealing himself to men. No amount of human striving could purchase the redemption or justification that man seeks.

This is the message that Latin America needs; it is the message of the risen Christ, the culmination of God's act of redemption and reconciliation, a message of power to make all things new — mind, will, and heart, even life itself.

IX

Faith in Action

THE GREAT PARADE

From April 29 to May 5, 1957, the Protestant churches of Guatemala celebrated the diamond jubilee of the Protestant work that began in 1882.[1] Each night during the week a mass meeting was held in a large open-air theater in the capital city, its use having been authorized by the President of the republic for this purpose. The main speakers at these meetings were Dr. John A. Mackay, president of Princeton Theological Seminary and for forty years a recognized authority on Latin American culture, and Dr. Alfonso Rodríguez, president of Union Theological Seminary at Matanzas, Cuba — a brilliant spokesman for Latin American Protestantism.

The climax of the celebrations came on Sunday, May 5, when a gigantic procession of Evangelicals passed through the main street of the city. The secular press estimated the number who took part in this event at 100,000 people; the procession stretched from one end of Guatemala City to the other. One newspaper correspondent, commenting in a daily newspaper, said it not only had great religious significance, but it was also an important civic act. In a sense it was a celebration of the granting of religious freedom in Guatemala by President Rufino Barrios a few years before he invited the Presbyterian Board to send missionaries to his country. Another newspaper reporter was impressed by the fact that members of the organizing committee for the procession stationed themselves at street intersections and every now and again held up the parade momentarily to allow the cross traffic of the city to go through. He felt that this demonstration of civic responsibility was something rather unusual.

Who were the people who took part in this parade? They were the Evangelicals belonging to various denominations and groups, who had come by car, by bus, by train, and on foot from all over Guatemala for this mass demonstration of Protestant faith. There were the rural people — men and women with toil-worn hands and the look of the soil about them; Indian women in colorful native costume, carrying bundles on their heads and babies strapped to their backs. There were the townspeople, all kinds of them — the middle-class folk and the upper classes, the artisans, the poor. There were school children marching precisely in their neat uniforms. There were the very young, the mature, the old. They rode in cars, on motorcycles, and on bicycles, but most of them walked. They came in groups according to their local church or organization, carrying banners and singing hymns, raising their voices in paeans of praise, marching, marching with buoyant and confident step, testifying to the power of Christ in their lives.

Late in the afternoon the procession reached the great open park, Campo de Marte, where the main address was delivered by Dr. Rodríguez, who took as his text Paul's words " I know whom I have believed." He said that one of the tragedies of the Latin American people is that for centuries they have known only a caricature of Jesus Christ and that is why there is such widespread superstition on the one hand and lack of faith on the other.

This celebration, and especially the great parade of May 5, were a demonstration of the vigor and numerical strength of the Evangelical churches in Guatemala; this same vitality and growth is to be found in other countries in Latin America.

In 1916 there was an Evangelical community (i.e., members and adherents) of 122,875,[2] in all Latin America. In 1956, forty years later, there were forty times as many, it being estimated that there were five million Evangelicals. With over two million people who call themselves Protestants in Brazil, the movement has grown faster percentagewise in that country than in any other part of the world except Korea.

In 1955, Father Vergara, a Jesuit priest in Chile, published an article entitled " El Avance de los Evangélicos en Chile " (The Growth of the Evangelical Movement in Chile), in which he stated that there were 681,770 Evangelicals in Chile, or 11.36 per cent of the entire population, while an optimistic estimate of Chileans who attend Mass was only 10 per cent. Of the total number of Evangelicals, 400,000 were Pentecostals. Father Vergara referred to the strong sense of evangelistic mission among the Evangelicals, particularly the Pentecostals, stressing the way in which their influence is felt among their neighbors, at work and at play, in street preaching and evangelism in general.

Protestantism is now an indigenous movement in Latin America, with strong " national " churches (i.e, independent of foreign control in any way), institutions, and trained leadership.

" A CHOSEN GENERATION, . . . A PECULIAR PEOPLE "

One of the richest passages in the Bible is to be found in The First Epistle General of Peter. Writing to " the strangers scattered throughout Pontus, Galatia, Cappadocia, Asia, and Bithynia " (I Peter 1:1), i.e., to the Christian congregations there, he says, " Ye also, as lively stones, are built up a spiritual house, a holy priesthood " (I Peter 2:5). In this building the chief cornerstone, the stone to which all the others are related, is Jesus Christ.

In passing, let us note that Peter speaks of a holy priesthood; later on he calls it a " royal priesthood." In other words, Peter believed in the principle of the priesthood of all believers, since he was referring to all the Christians of the areas mentioned. He goes on to say, " But ye are a chosen generation, a royal priesthood, a holy nation, a peculiar people; that ye should show forth the praises of him who hath called you out of darkness into his marvelous light: which in time past were not a people, but are now the people of God: which had not obtained mercy, but now have obtained mercy " (I Peter 2:9-10).

This passage is also a description of the groups of Evangelicals in twenty Latin American countries, who form the holy nation, or peculiar people, numbering over five million. These people have some common cultural ties and background: there is the racial background, Indian, mestizo, Spanish, or Portuguese; there is the language relationship, whether it be Spanish or Portuguese; and there is a common heritage of struggle for political freedom. Across all lines of nationality and culture, the Evangelicals of the twenty countries are bound together most of all by a common loyalty to Jesus Christ. There is a growing sense of their belonging together; more and more they feel they are an Evangelical nation. The word " nation " comes from the Latin *natus,* which is the past participle of *nasci,* to be born, and the Evangelical nation is the vast company of those who have been " born again." Before they were born into this new life they were just people, belonging to this country or that, but now they are people of God, having obtained mercy.

Peter uses the phrase " a chosen generation " or " the elect " to signify those who have been called from darkness into light for a purpose.

The use of the word " decision " in evangelism has given the impression that a Christian convert is one who decides to be on the side of Christ, one who " chooses " Christ. The element of decision is more accurately described as a response to a call. Christ said, " Ye have not chosen me, but I have chosen you " (John 15:16). It is in this sense that those who become Christians or servants of the Lord are set apart. For what are these people called, or chosen? Peter answers that question himself when he says " that ye should show forth the praises of him who hath called you out of darkness into his marvelous light " (I Peter 2:9). The words " show forth the praises " form one of the luminous phrases of the Scriptures, rich in meaning and significance.

The word " salvation " connotes being saved from something, particularly the consequences of sin; it also carries with it an obligation, namely, being saved for something. Faith must be dynamic; salvation is *for* something.

Peter describes the priestly function of the individual Christians when he says that they are " to offer up spiritual sacrifices, acceptable to God by Jesus Christ" (I Peter 2:5). Thus the first obligation upon a Christian is to live a life of sacrifice for his ideals. "If any man will come after me, let him deny himself, and take up his cross, and follow me" (Matt. 16:24).

THE PROCLAMATION OF THE GOSPEL

The first obligation of the church is to proclaim the gospel. The Biblical view of the church is that it is the body of believers, or a fellowship, and that it is the body of Christ, as Paul puts it. Moreover, salvation does not depend on, or derive from, the church; Jesus Christ is the Savior, not the church. This fundamental distinction regarding the nature and function of the church and the message it proclaims is very important in Latin America.

The view expounded from the pulpit of St. Patrick's Cathedral, New York, by Rev. Bernard P. Donachie, is that "the Catholic Church claims to be Christ. She acts like Christ and she can prove from Scripture that she is Christ."[3] The Protestant or Evangelical viewpoint is radically different from this: it is that the church is the body of Christ and that Christ is the head. This divergence of concepts of the nature of the church has a profound influence on the work and message of the Christian church. "In the Roman view," says Dr. Mackay, "Jesus Christ has virtually abdicated. He has handed over to the church, and particularly to the pope, his vicar or vicegerent, all things relating to the affairs of his church upon earth."[4]

When a Latin American accepts Christ and becomes an Evangelical Christian, he must also be instructed concerning the true nature of the church as the body of Christ. Essential as organization and institutional life are, the church is primarily a fellowship and as such it is also an instrument for the extension of Christ's Kingdom.

THE LIFE OF THE CHURCHES

Before considering the task of evangelism in Latin America, we must pause to look at the churches themselves.

The local church is the basis of the strategy of the Christian movement. The body of Christ is composed of cells which are the local churches. When the local churches lose their vitality, then the life of the body as a whole is weakened. The spiritual life of the local church must be nourished by constant communion with Christ who is the head of the church, by a deep devotional life and by an effective witness in the community. When the church becomes an institution and loses its spiritual life and vigor, then it ceases to be a church as the fellowship of believers banded together so that they might show forth the praises of the Lord. The local church must always be growing and renewing its life, like a living cell.

Local churches must find new ways in which their members may witness in their communities. Each local church should have a dynamic missionary program which can challenge the laity and enlist their active participation. Too often a new member is expected to assume a merely passive role in the life of the church, and has no opportunity either to serve or to grow spiritually. He must be inspired to take part in programs of evangelism, human betterment, and civic welfare, going forth into the community with a new sense of commitment and responsibility. For this he must have special training.

The churches, in other words, must not withdraw within themselves and develop an in-group complex. They must live on the frontiers of life with a dynamic sense of mission.

What about the relation of the local churches with those of other denominations or groups? There should be some form of co-operation both at the local and national levels. The witness of the Christian church is being limited, and even hurt, by the lack of co-operation among Evangelicals (although significant progress toward better understanding among various groups has been made in recent years). National Evangelical councils are performing a service to the Christian cause which would be difficult for any one group to render.

During recent years the development of independent sects and faith missions has been quite marked in Latin America; it is undoubtedly true that a large part of the numerical growth of Protestantism in recent years has been due to their intense evangelistic efforts. The number of missionaries under the independent groups has increased beyond that of the denominations or regular mission boards, probably because the latter have sought in every way possible to develop national leadership by diverting funds for this purpose and also by turning over responsibility to national churches. (It should, however, be mentioned that some of the independent groups, such as the Pentecostals in Chile, are completely indigenous, that is, they have developed without the help of funds and personnel from abroad.) While the denominations have fostered more the growth of indigenous leadership and the national churches, the faith groups and independent missionaries have often shown commendable evangelical warmth and zeal.

This diversity of sects, while primarily' based on the fundamental Protestant principle of freedom of interpretation, has laid the Protestant movement open to criticism from various sources, the charge being made that there is no doctrinal unity and sense of direction.

What, then, is the answer? On the one hand there is the Roman Catholic Church, claiming to be the only true Christian church, with a unified command and a more or less monolithic organization, and on the other, the multiple sects and denominational groups. Must these groups now come together in one great Protestant Church? Sincere Protestants are divided on this big issue, and there are strong feelings on both sides. This is not the place to debate it, and nothing would be gained by doing so. Without claiming prophetic powers, we can venture to state that organic church union, even on a small scale, will not take place so easily in Latin America as in other parts of the world. The answer seems to be co-operation on a voluntary basis, i.e., united action on certain phases of Evangelical work. One of the imperatives in the years ahead is for some common goals and strategy, as well as mutual understanding, to be worked out between these two large over-all groups without the need for any elaborate organizational relationship. The greatness of the task and the opportunities in Latin America demand this. The genius of Protestantism, with its emphasis on private judgment, is that there are different interpretations and viewpoints; but if diverse groups can work together and present a common front on certain essentials of Christian witness, then they will honor their common Lord and demonstrate in an eloquent way, so that the world might believe, that there is an overarching loyalty to Jesus Christ which binds them together as Christians.

EVANGELISM — HOW?

From the days of the early Christian church to modern times, the most common method of spreading the gospel has been that of speaking from the Word of God to the multitude or the group, large or small. This is being done in Latin America in churches, halls, and — in the countries that permit it — in the market place. The gospel message has been preached in organized campaigns with great effectiveness in many parts of Latin America. Commemorations of important events in the life of the churches have been used as occasions for evangelistic thrusts. In 1949, the Evangelicals of Puerto Rico celebrated the fiftieth anniversary of the founding of Protestant work in that country, with a great rally in the big San Juan stadium. In 1956, all the churches joined the Presbyterians in Colombia in marking the one hundredth anniversary of their work by a series of evangelistic meetings in various cities. Mexican Evangelicals honored their diamond jubilee several years ago with evangelistic goals and campaigns, and other groups are preparing similar celebrations in the next few years.

Besides the evangelistic campaign which is quite common in Latin America and has achieved notable results, the value of other means such as personal evangelism and newspaper evangelism must not be overlooked. The laity can be enlisted in these types of work, and the churches should provide adequate preparation for their participation. There are also other media for communicating the gospel message which should be utilized to a much greater extent than has been done in the past. These media are literature, drama, radio, television, and visual aids. Although there is often a tendency for each denominational group to develop its own program independently of others, these media of communication are of such a nature that they can be more effectively, and more economically, used by the pooling of resources of various groups in a co-operative program. Outstanding examples are the programs developed by literature committees under the various Evangelical councils with local funds and those supplied by mission boards, through the Committee on Cooperation in Latin America. Another example, the audio-visual center, known as CAVE (Centro Audio Visual Evangélico), serves a number of different groups in Brazil, providing them with excellent radio programs, filmstrips, slides, and so on, for use in their churches. The Cadena Cultural Panamericana (Pan-American Christian Network) is also performing a valuable service by supplying radio programs in Spanish to Evangelical broadcasting stations in various countries. The churches must become aware of the development in these media of communication in the secular world, and they must realize that radio programs, motion pictures, dramas, and books are to be of high quality if they are to make any real impact.

The opportunities for proclaiming the gospel in Latin America are perhaps greater than in any other major area of the world. The living Christ alone can satisfy the deep longings of the heart and supply the spiritual needs of the Latin American people, who have grown tired of and disillusioned with ecclesiasticism.

Evangelism —for Whom?

The gospel is the story of good news for all men everywhere, and the only limitations to its widespread dissemination are the inadequacies and lack of resources of the churches themselves.

In Latin America, strategy demands that special efforts be made to reach certain groups because of the growing part they play in society. These groups are: intellectuals, university students, youth, and industrial workers.

The Latin American intellectuals, as a group, are difficult to reach with the Christian message. The search of the intellectual for truth is largely rational; he requires positive proof or certainty, and it is difficult to convince him that there is another approach to truth and belief, namely, through experience. At the same time, the intellectual very often is a man with a deep spiritual hunger, who is willing to attend popular lectures in halls or universities to listen to men like John A. Mackay, Alfonso Rodríguez, Alberto, Rembao, George P. Howard, Miguel Rizzo, Gonzalo Baez Camargo, and Cecilio Arrastía.

Dr. Miguel Rizzo, who for years has conducted what he calls the Instituto de Cultura Religiosa (Institute of Religious Culture) in Brazil — which arranges for popular lectures on religious subjects — was called to Rio de Janeiro soon after the Eucharistic Congress was held in that city in July, 1955, by a Roman Catholic layman who had been prominent in the organization of that congress. The layman had, by chance, read a tract on " Communion with God " written by Dr. Rizzo and, upon making inquiries, he had found out who the author was and where he could be reached. He offered Dr. Rizzo time on the radio station he controlled so that he could broadcast his message to the Brazilian people.

In Colombia, some years ago, a missionary made personal contact with professional men, lawyers, doctors, and professors, inviting them to his home to discuss the Christian gospel. Out of this personal work there came an active group of devoted Christian men.

As we have already noted, the impact of Evangelical schools and homes has produced professionals and intellectuals who find no difficulty in identifying themselves with a Protestant congregation. It is to these men and women that we look for leadership in the Protestant movement. The intellectuals we have discussed above are those who, nurtured in the principles and practices of the Roman Catholic Church, have turned their back on these, and find themselves in a spiritual vacuum. This group, although receptive to the Christian message when presented by another intellectual, are reluctant to participate in any forms of worship that might be even faintly reminiscent of those they have discarded. Coupled with this situation is a fear of social and political ostracism.

University students also have an intellectual approach to life; as a group they are of strategic importance to the Protestant movement. Evangelical work among university students has developed greatly in recent years under the auspices of the interdenominational World Student Christian Federation. Two factors have tended to account for the progress made: first of all, the appointment of a full-time Secretary for Student Work in Latin America in 1953, and, secondly, the holding of several student training institutes, thus providing local leadership in the various countries. A new development which will have great significance for the student movement in Latin America, as well as the rest of the world, is the study by student groups of the nature and place of the Christian church. In the meantime, with the establishment in some of the Latin American capitals of what are called "University Cities," a new impetus has been given to student life and the opportunities for student Christian centers have been enlarged.

Similarly, the Evangelical youth program has had far-reaching importance with the holding of periodic youth conferences under the Latin American youth organization known as ULAJE (Unión Latinoamericana de Juventudes Evangélicas). As Latin American youth faces some of the great issues of the day in the light of the Christian gospel, the Evangelical churches are beginning to reflect their influence, for as time goes on these young people tend to occupy positions of leadership in the church.

Another group that is of strategic importance in Latin America and must be challenged by the Christian gospel are the industrial workers, who, up to now, are largely unreached. We have seen in an earlier chapter how industrialization has been accelerated in recent years and how the number of industrial workers has increased in the cities and towns.

The Latin American Evangelical Conference held in Buenos Aires in 1949 studied the causes of the estrangement of the masses from the Roman Catholic Church. They found they were: the indifference of the church in the face of exploitation and oppression by the privileged classes and the big landholders; the tendency to give more importance to charity than to social justice; and the preaching of submission and resignation to one's lot on earth, with the promise that things will be brighter in the hereafter.

Catholic Action is trying to remedy this situation in some countries. In Peru, Miss Rosario Araoz conducts one of the best social programs in Latin America, according to Father Albert J. Nevins. "We have five main classes of problems in Peru," Miss Araoz explains. "First, illiteracy; second, low cultural life; third, family instability; fourth, urban housing; and fifth, special rural problems. We are approaching all of these problems from spiritual principles." [5]

Father Nevins observes that Catholic social leaders are few and far between; "they stand out like beacons in the night." Bishop Manuel Lorrain in Chile is one of these, and he has encouraged the formation of industrial and agricultural unions in his diocese. "Because he implemented the encyclicals," says Father Nevins, "he was accused of being a Red." [6] In a forthright manner Father Nevins charges the most ardent churchgoers in Peru of being the leading oppressors of the poor. Through their wealth, he says, they have power to silence any opposition.

What about the attitude of the Evangelical churches toward the working classes? One of the papers read at the Evangelical Conference of Buenos Aires in 1949 said that "the workers view the Evangelical churches with the same indifference and in some cases with the same antagonistic spirit as they view the Church of Rome." [7] The statement went on to say that the tendency in Protestant churches in Latin America is to form a middle class composed of semiprofessional, white-collar, employee-type people.

In Brazil, an ecumenical team of five young men began a new type of experiment and experience. In the team were a graduate student of sociology, a Presbyterian minister, a Methodist minister from Uruguay, a teacher, and a factory worker who was an industrial leader. They obtained employment in different factories in order to gain experience and understanding of the workers' point of view and also as a means of coming in close contact with them through identification.

The Evangelical churches must find ways of making an effective approach to industrial workers so that they may understand the implications of the Christian gospel and know that the Christian church is on the side of social justice and righteousness.

SERVING HUMAN NEEDS

The Christian church has always endeavored to express the spirit of the Master by ministering to human need in its many forms. The gospel of Christ is related to the whole of life, and whether it be relieving human suffering through medical care, improving home and family life, redeeming the land, or educating the young, the church has a responsibility.

American and British medical missionaries have rendered valuable service in a number of countries in Latin America, at great personal sacrifice. They belong to the noble band of unsung heroes of the modern missionary enterprise. Besides alleviating human suffering and combating disease, they have made a unique contribution in several countries to the medical profession by establishing nursing schools. Due to the influence of Evangelical doctors, nursing is becoming a dignified vocation for young women, and the graduates of these schools are greatly in demand in government and private institutions. In many cases Latin American Protestant doctors are foregoing the larger remuneration of a private medical practice to render devoted service in hospitals under Evangelical auspices.

Another facet of the work of the Evangelical churches is the improvement of home and family life — of undisputed significance to any nation. This is a task to which women's groups in many countries have dedicated their energies with zeal. The promotion of a healthy family and a happy home life is an ideal that women's organizations have set before them. Acute problems are to be found in these fields among the poorer classes in urban areas and among rural people. Women's work in its organized form is an increasingly important part of the life and program of the church in Latin America.

As we have seen, the majority of the population in Latin America derive their livelihood from the soil. Rural people are poor and lack the resources, as well as the knowledge, necessary for bettering the conditions under which they live. Rural missions include every effort to bring the gospel to bear on the problems of rural life in an attempt to uplift people by improving their physical surroundings. Involved in rural programs is the redemption of the land itself so that it may become more productive. Farmers must be introduced to improved agricultural and stock-raising methods, taught how to prevent soil erosion, how to fertilize, and the use of better seeds. Above all, they must learn to help themselves in order to maintain their dignity as human beings. Evangelical churches in Latin America are beginning to realize that they must train more workers, pastors, laymen, and laywomen for service in the name of Christ to people living in rural communities.

One of the most important contributions of the Evangelical movement to the life and culture of Latin America is in the field of education; some of the finest institutions are under its auspices. It is noteworthy that in a number of countries educational missionaries from North America have been decorated by governments for their service to the people. Evangelicals believe in putting educational opportunities within the reach of all; through scholarship funds they have helped poor parents send their children to school. In the field of higher education and with eventual Christian service in mind, mission boards have granted scholarships to promising young men and women to pursue graduate studies in the United States.

The Evangelical churches in Latin America — and the mission boards that supply the funds for the purpose — believe that education should be based on Christian principles and emphasize the development of character as a preparation for life. Many of the leaders in the churches in Latin America today, as well as men prominent in business, professional, and public life, have been educated in Protestant schools.

THE SOCIAL RESPONSIBILITY OF THE CHURCH

The Christian church can no longer avoid its responsibility in society if it is to be true to its Lord, the head of the church. It must face the larger issues that confront people everywhere.

The Protestant viewpoint is that the Christian church should not " mix in politics "; it should neither align itself with any political party or economic system, nor use politics to bolster up its own authority and power. What then should be the relationship of the church to the political and economic life of society? The Christian church should, in the first place, be the conscience of society, and it cannot be true to itself and remain indifferent to exploitation, social injustice, political oppression, and the suppression of human rights and freedom. In Latin America, up to now, the Evangelical churches have largely limited what we might call their social action to the struggle for religious freedom and human rights.

The role of the Evangelical churches, then, in Latin America, should be to help create " a responsible society." The Amsterdam Assembly of the World Council of Churches defined the responsible society as one where " freedom is the freedom of men who acknowledge responsibility to justice and public order, and where those who hold public authority or economic power are responsible for its exercise to God and the people whose welfare is affected by it."

There are those in the secular world who seek some of the goals of a responsible society, but they do so from different motives and start from different premises. The Christian church starts from the concept of God's will for men. It is not the will of God that some human beings, or groups, should exploit others, and it is not the will of God that social injustice should prevail, or that the conscience of anyone be shackled or his personality violated. The Christian church believes that through faith and salvation in Christ, man turns away from the self-interest that poisons and distorts social life and strives to serve his neighbors in love.

" Faith is the only source of responsible action which does not dry up in the face of guilt and the inescapable consequences of established fact, since it does not spring from human vitality but from the grace of God himself. Where man knows to whom he is responsible, even in the grip of circumstances not of his own making, he is able to take responsible action." [8]

In Brazil some Evangelical leaders realized in 1955 that the churches had given very little evidence of their concern for social and political problems, and as a consequence the laymen of the church saw little or no relationship between Christian faith and political action. In that year a group of prominent church leaders came together to study the social responsibility of the church as well as the effects of rapid social change on urban and rural communities. A study department with a Commission on Church and Society has been formed under the auspices of the Evangelical Confederation of Brazil.

The first studies centered around the Biblical and theological foundations of Christian participation in society and the current situation in Brazil. Three working groups have been formed within the Commission, namely, political, industrial, and rural. Thus a beginning has been made in this very important field of studying the implications of the Christian gospel in the social, economic, and political life of Brazil.

An Indigenous Church in a New Day

The significance of the coming into existence of a world-wide church was highlighted in 1942 by the late Archbishop Temple when he referred to it as the " great new fact of our time."

The development of the Evangelical churches of Latin America is also one of the great new facts of our time. Lacking in resources for the task before them, and in some cases a struggling minority, yet always a minority, these churches hold the promise of a new day in Latin America, for they have vigor and vitality.

North American and British mission boards and societies sent their missionaries to preach the gospel and to live the Christian life among the people of Latin America during the past hundred years. The seed planted faithfully in the hearts of the people took root and began to grow. In the last twenty-five or thirty years the harvest has been truly plentiful. Churches have developed and reached independence and self-support; more and more they have become part of the world-wide Christian fellowship as their representatives have participated in world gatherings. Mission boards have welcomed this growth and development of the churches, and some of them have come to see that the words " foreign " and " missions " have no longer a rightful place in the world-wide movement. Increasingly they refer to the ecumenical mission of the church, which means that all churches are engaged in the great task of evangelizing the world together and making Jesus Christ regnant in the hearts and lives of all men everywhere. As more committed Christians catch the vision of the mission of the church in the world and explore imaginatively new ways of serving Christ, the task seems to grow larger and become more compelling.

When North American Christians and Latin American Christians alike come to realize a togetherness in a great common undertaking, and are willing to share experience, know-how, and resources, then they come closer to one another as brothers in Christ.

The new day and the development of the indigenous church may mean a shift in emphasis in the role of missionaries; they may be called upon to take secondary places in the work of the churches or in institutions, under national leaders. Sometimes the most fruitful Christian service a missionary or fraternal worker [9] can render in such circumstances is to labor in the spirit of the Master, who said that the greatest in the Kingdom are those who serve without any thought of reward.

Let it be said, however, that the indigenous church is not an end in itself; it cannot isolate itself from the rest of the world. Experience in recent years has shown that when a so-called " younger church," which has developed under the leadership of the missionary movement, reaches maturity and independence, it seeks fellowship with other members of the body of Christ. A new togetherness is felt and a wider community of interests is developed; the churches are eager to share their problems, their joys, and their aspirations.

The message of the consultation of the Presbyterian churches held at Lake Mohonk in May, 1956, had this to say: "We have come together from churches in many lands. In some lands Christ as Lord is being freely proclaimed; in others his claims are fiercely resisted, and his followers endure ignominy, suffering, and even death for his sake. . . . In our fellowship here we have had wonderful things to tell each other of triumphant experiences in Christ."

The indigenous church as part of the ecumenical mission of the church now takes its place alongside the older churches, entering into a vital encounter with the world in the name of Jesus Christ. In addition, the Evangelical churches of Latin America can learn much from each other, since there are various stages of development in the different countries.

Latin American Protestants have much to contribute to the world-wide church. There is a natural, emotional warmth in the expression of their faith and witness, which is both contagious and exhilarating. The Latin American brings into his Christian life some of the psychological characteristics that we studied in a previous chapter, such as individualism, personalism, formality, and friendliness. Christian truth in Latin America must be personal. Cold, rational presentations will never win people to Christ, but winsome, radiant Christian personalities can. Besides an emotional warmth, there is a strong evangelical note in Latin American Protestantism and a spirit that is very similar to that of the Reformation.

A New Reformation

What form Protestantism will take in Latin America in the years ahead, we do not know. The growing Latin American churches themselves, it is hoped, will develop in a way that is consonant with the qualities of heart and mind of the Latin American peoples. In other words, no reproduction of North American or European church life, its institutions and practices, or its interpretation of Christian principles and beliefs will supply the answer to Latin American problems.

Furthermore, a re-enactment of the sixteenth-century Reformation, in the same form and manner, would be an anachronism and fail to create a movement adequate for Latin America in the twentieth century. What Latin America needs, however, is a New Reformation, a Reformation that will bear the marks of its own genius, gifts, attitudes, and aspirations. This Reformation has already begun, and as it continues to spread in the hearts of the people, it will create a dynamic Christian faith with a spiritual power and vision, as well as moral purpose.

The Living Christ in a New Day

The task facing the Evangelical churches in Latin America in the years ahead is a challenging task of vast dimensions. They must ever be on their guard against institutionalism, rigidity, and the temptation to become ingrown. The church of Jesus Christ must be a crusading one, moving under his banner and leadership, out on the new frontiers of life.

Necessary as church organization and institutionalism are, they must ever be subordinate to the vital spiritual life of the church and to the Lordship of Christ. Leaders with the best training and preparation are greatly needed; yet the work of the Kingdom will largely depend on the quality of the witness of the rank and file, the laymen and laywomen, and on their loyalty to Christ in daily living.

A dynamic faith that will send men and women forth to win others and to challenge the forces of evil and darkness must be Christ-centered. This is the message that Latin America needs today, the message of a living Christ who can transform life, both of the individual and of the community. No religion, no matter how elaborate and aesthetic, and no ecclesiastical system, however powerful, can lead Latin America toward a new day of justice, righteousness, freedom, understanding, and love. The power of the living Christ alone, untrammeled and free to work in the hearts of men, can purify, inspire, energize, and enable.

Christ must be in all and through all, the beginning and the end. The Christian life begins when a person is called to follow Christ; it is a response to the divine impulse. Following him as living Lord involves an attitude of learning, which is the essence of discipleship. Christ said that unless we become as little children, we cannot enter the Kingdom of God. Becoming a disciple of Christ means loyalty to him, the fulfilling of his commandments, a closeness to the Master, and an intimate companionship which he himself likened to the relationship of the branch to the vine. The price of discipleship and loyalty to Christ is a cross.

The Christian must also be a witness to the living Christ in a new day, when so many siren voices are being heard, and the forces that would enslave men's minds and bring them into subjection are felt on all sides. Witnessing, as we have seen, is at the heart of Protestantism, and it takes two forms: first, as a personal testimony of the power of Christ, speaking out of one's own experience; and secondly, as a witness in the community; in other words, faith in action, a dynamic faith that can change society, as well as man himself.

Amid all the changes, economic, social, and political, that are taking place in Latin America today, man himself is the chief problem, for without new men in Christ, with a dynamic faith and a moral and spiritual purpose, Latin America cannot solve its outstanding problems or fulfill its destiny in a new day of promise and opportunity.

Notes

Chapter I. Ideological Mainstreams

[1] Richard Pattee, *Catholicism in Latin America*, p. 9.

[2] R. H. Tawney, *Religion and the Rise of Capitalism*, p. 110.

[3] *Ibid.*, p. 42.

[4] Julio Navarro Monzó, *The Religious Problem in Latin American Culture*, p. 42.

[5] Américo Castro, *The Structure of Spanish History*, p. 130.

[6] Claudio Gutiérrez Marín, *Historia de la Reforma en España*, p. 32.

[7] We are indebted for this section to Claudio Gutiérrez Marín, *op. cit.*, pp. 101–114.

[8] Jacques Delpech, *The Oppression of Protestants in Spain*, pp. 6–7.

[9] Waldo Frank, *South of Us*, p. 316.

[10] *Ibid.*, p. 315.

[11] Navarro Monzó, *op. cit.*, pp. 45–46.

[12] W. R. Inge, *The Church in the World*, p. 53.

CHAPTER II. THE LATIN AMERICAN SCENE TODAY

[1] Quoted by Germán Arciniegas, *Green Continent*, p. 27.

[2] Luis Quintanilla, *A Latin American Speaks*, p. 73

[3] Agnese Lockwood, *Indians of the Andes*, p. 410.

[4] *Population of South America, 1950–1980* and *Population of Central America, 1950–1980*, United Nations, Bureau of Social Affairs, Population Branch, 1955.

[5] Willard R. Espy, *Bold New Program*, p. 92.

[6] *Latin American Business Highlights*, Chase Manhattan Bank, September, 1955, p. 1.

[7] *Ibid.*

[8] Espy, *op. cit.*, p. 89.

[9] Quoted by Samuel Guy Inman, " The Impact of the Modern World on Latin America — A Politico-Economic and Technological Approach," *Civilisations* (Quarterly), Vol. V (1955), No. 4, p. 558.

[10] Germán Arciniegas, *The State of Latin America*, p. 389.

[11] Manoel da Nóbrega, *Demagogia Política e Religiosa*, p. 62.

[12] Arciniegas, *The State of Latin America*.

[13] César Barros Hurtado, *América — Penurias de Libertad,* pp. 18 ff.

[14] Julio Navarro Monzó, *The Religious Problem in Latin American Culture,* p. 35.

CHAPTER III. RACIAL, CULTURAL, AND POLITICAL PATTERNS

[1] Carlos Octavio Bunge, *Nuestra América,* p. 49.

[2] Samuel Guy Inman, *Latin America, Its Place in World Life,* p. 44.

[3] Vianna Moog, *Bandeirantes e Pioneiros: Paralelo Entre Duas Culturas,* p. 105.

[4] Salvador de Madariaga, *Englishmen, Frenchmen and Spaniards,* p. 4.

[5] By "passion" is meant fervor or continuous emotional intensity.

[6] Madariaga, *op. cit.,* p. 108.

[7] John A. Mackay, *The Other Spanish Christ,* p. 4.

[8] *Ibid.,* p. 17.

[9] Lewis Hanke, *Bartolomé de las Casas — Pensador Político, Historiador, Antropólogo,* p. 38.

[10] *Ibérica,* July 15, 1956, p. 5.

[11] Erico Verissimo, *Brazilian Literature,* p. 6.

[12] From APRA, the initials of Alianza Popular Revolucionaria Americana (American Popular Revolutionary Alliance).

[13] Gustavo Adolfo Otero, *Figura y Carácter del Indio*, p. 176.

[14] Robert Allen Christopher, " The Human Race in Brazil," *Américas,* Vol. 5, No. 7, July, 1953, p. 5.

[15] Gilberto Freyre, *Brazil, an Interpretation*, p. 95.

[16] Quoted by Fernando de Azevedo, *Brazilian Culture*, p. 122.

[17] See note 12 above.

[18] The preceding section owes much to the ideas developed by Professor F. S. C. Northrop in a paper read at a Study Conference at the Kennedy School of Missions in May, 1955, entitled " The Struggle for Order and Progress," and published in *Civilisations* (Quarterly), Vol. V (1955), No. 4, p. 525.

[19] Auguste Comte (1798–1857) was the founder of the system of philosophy called positivism. It is based on a purely scientific and humanistic view of life which excludes everything except natural phenomena.

[20] Alfonso López Michelsen, *La Estripe Calvinista de Nuestras Instituciones*.

[21] F. García Calderón, *Latin America, Its Rise and Progress*, p. 240.

CHAPTER IV. PRE-COLUMBIAN RELIGIONS

[1] Mathew W. Sterling, *Indians of the Americas*, p. 215.

[2] G. C. Vaillant, *The Aztecs of Mexico*, pp. 179–181.

[3] Shamanism is a primitive religion in which only the priest, or shaman, has access to the hidden world of deities, spirits, and demons.

[4] The emperor was known as " the Inca."

[5] W. H. Prescott, *Conquest of Peru,* p. 70.

CHAPTER V. THE CONQUISTADORES — SPAIN OR GOD?

[1] Quoted by Lewis Hanke, *Bartolomé de las Casas — Pensador Político,* p. 7.

[2] F. D. David, *Our Neighbors of the Andes,* p. 16.

[3] The " White Legend," as contrasted to the " Black Legend," is the thesis upheld by some writers and historians that Spain's role in the development of its conquered territories in the New World was a Christian and magnanimous one that did it honor.

[4] Salvador de Madariaga, *The Rise of the Spanish American Empire,* Prologue, p. xv.

[5] Mariano Picón y Salas, *De la Conquista a la Independencia,* p. 40.

[6] Madariaga, *op. cit.,* and *The Fall of the Spanish American Empire.*

[7] See Chapter III.

[8] Madariaga, *The Fall of the Spanish American Empire,* p. 16.

[9] Madariaga, *The Rise of the Spanish American Empire,* p. 14.

[10] *Ibid.,* p. 37.

[11] *Ibid.,* p. 159.

[12] *Ibid.,* p. 165.

[13] Hanke, *Bartolomé de las Casas — Pensador Político,* pp. 56–57.

[14] Hanke, *Bartolomé de las Casas — Historian,* p. 73.

[15] *Ibid.,* p. 96.

[16] Hanke, *Bartolomé de las Casas — Pensador Político,* Prologue, p. xxxix.

[17] Hanke, *Bartolomé de las Casas — Historian.*

[18] An "encomienda" was a commandery of so many Indians given to a Spaniard along with lands granted by the King of Spain. The recipient, or *encomendero,* was "to teach them things of our Holy Catholic faith."

[19] Hanke, *Bartolomé de las Casas — Pensador Político,* pp. 19–21.

[20] *Ibid.,* Prologue, p. xiv.

[21] *Ibid.,* p. 25.

[22] David Jenks, *Six Great Missionaries of the Sixteenth–Seventeenth Centuries,* p. 34.

[23] Bernard Moses, *South America on the Eve of Emancipation,* p. 120.

[24] Bailey W. Diffie, *Latin American Civilization*, p. 246.

[25] Hanke, *Bartolomé de las Casas — Pensador Político*, Prologue, p. xxxi.

CHAPTER VI. FROM PAGANISM TO ROMAN CATHOLICISM

[1] Robertson, *América*, Vol. III, p. 5. (Quoted by W. H. Prescott, *Conquest of Peru*, p. 143.)

[2] W. H. Prescott, *op. cit.*, p. 246.

[3] *Ibid.*, p. 250.

[4] *Ibid.*, p. 251.

[5] Silvio Zavala, *New Viewpoints on the Spanish Colonization of America*, p. 7.

[6] *Ibid.*, p. 8.

[7] Clericalism, according to Dr. John A. Mackay, is " the pursuit of power, especially political power, by a religious hierarchy, carried on by secular methods for purposes of social domination." " Our Future as Protestants," *Presbyterian Life*, January 6, 1951, p. 8.

[8] Hubert Herring, *A History of Latin America*, p. 181.

[9] Prescott, *op. cit.*, p. 260.

[10] Fray Toribio de Benavente (Motolinía), *Relaciones de la Nueva España*, Prologue, p. xxxvi.

[11] John Collier and Aníbal Buitrón, *The Awakening Valley*, p. 95.

[12] Alberto Rembao, " Pre-Hispanic Religion in Modern Mexico," *International Review of Missions,* April, 1942, p. 166.

[13] Collier and Buitrón, *op. cit.,* p. 101.

[14] Rembao, *loc. cit.,* p. 167.

[15] Anita Brenner, *Idols Behind Altars,* p. 132.

[16] Quoted by Rembao, *loc. cit.,* p. 167.

[17] Oscar Lewis, *Life in a Mexican Village,* pp. 225–226.

[18] Julio Navarro Monzó, *Los Conceptos que de Cristo Tiene la América Latina,* p. 4.

[19] Fyodor Dostoevsky, *The Brothers Karamazov,* p. 305.

[20] *Ibid.,* pp. 307–308.

[21] *Ibid.,* p. 308–309.

[22] *Ibid.,* p. 313–315.

[23] Ricardo Rojas, *The Invisible Christ,* pp. 83–84.

[24] *Ibid.,* p. 17.

[25] *Ibid.,* p. 18.

[26] *Ibid.,* p. 285.

[27] Quoted by John A. Mackay, *The Other Spanish Christ,* p. 95.

[28] Mackay, *op. cit.,* p. 95.

[29] *Ibid.*, pp. 101–102.

[30] *Ibid.*, p. 102.

CHAPTER VII. RELIGIOUS CONDITIONS IN LATIN AMERICA TODAY

[1] W. S. Rycroft, editor, *Indians of the High Andes*, p. 300.

[2] Alcides Argüedas, *Pueblo Enfermo*, p. 43.

[3] Weston La Barre (quoted in *Indians of the High Andes*, W. S. Rycroft, editor, p. 127).

[4] J. Merle Davis, Unpublished manuscript.

[5] John Collier and Aníbal Buitrón, *The Awakening Valley*, p. 95.

[6] *Ibid.*, p. 100.

[7] Rycroft, editor, *op. cit.*, p. 136.

[8] Orlando Fals-Borda, *Peasant Society in the Colombian Andes*.

[9] *Ibid.*, pp. 220–221.

[10] *Ibid.*, p. 224.

[11] Name given to villagers living in Saucio.

[12] Fals-Borda, *op. cit.*, p. 223.

[13] *Ibid.*, p. 221.

[14] Mackay, *The Other Spanish Christ*, p. 97.

[15] Richard Pattee, "The Apostasy of the Masses," *The Holy Name Journal*, November 11, 1945.

[16] Gonzalo Baez Camargo, "A Roman Catholic Revival," *Christianity and Crisis*, September 29, 1952.

[17] Father Albert J. Nevins, "How Catholic Is Latin America?", *The Sign*, September, 1956.

[18] Ricardo Rojas, *The Invisible Christ*, p. 238.

[19] Julio Navarro Monzó, *The Religious Problem in Latin American Culture*, p. 85.

[20] *Ibid.*, p. 80.

[21] Nevins, *op. cit.*

[22] *Proceedings of the Lima Methods Conference of the Maryknoll Fathers*, p. 45.

[23] *Ibid.*, p. 9.

[24] The Treaty of Tordesillas, signed in 1494, settled the rival claims of the Spaniards and the Portuguese to newly discovered territories in the New World. An imaginary line, running from north to south, was drawn 400 leagues west of the Azores. Lands east of this line would belong to the Portuguese, and west of it, to the Spaniards. This treaty accounts for the fact that Brazil became Portuguese territory and that the other lands came under the sway of Spain.

[25] Erico Verissimo, *Brazilian Literature*, p. 5.

[26] Quoted by Fernando de Azevedo, *Brazilian Culture*, p. 140.

[27] Gilberto Freyre, *Brazil, an Interpretation,* p. 39.

[28] Charles H. Gauld, *Religion and Social Change,* unpublished manuscript, used with permission of the author.

[29] The term " Evangelical " is a generic term almost invariably used by the members of Protestant churches in Latin America. It is preferred because they wish it to be clearly understood that their message is a positive one (the evangel), and that the Evangelical movement is not merely a protest against Roman Catholicism. It is felt — rightly or wrongly — that the term " Protestant " has a negative connotation for some people. (The meaning of the word " Protestant " is discussed more fully in Chapter VIII.)

[30] The Evangelical Federation of Colombia (known as CEDEC, the initials of its name in Spanish) has compiled documentary evidence of several hundred of these incidents that have occurred since 1949.

[31] " La Iglesia en América Latina," *Problemas de Latinoamérica,* Vol. III, No. 11, February, 1956, p. 2.

[32] *Ibid.,* pp. 67–68.

CHAPTER VIII. RELIGION AND DYNAMIC FAITH

[1] Leonard D. Agate, *Luther and the Reformation,* p. 20.

[2] Karl Barth, *The Epistle to the Romans,* p. 248.

[3] *Ibid.,* p. 258.

[4] Hendrik Kraemer, *Religion and the Christian Faith,* p. 38.

[5] Quoted by John A. Mackay in *The Other Spanish Christ*, p. 262.

[6] Karl Barth, *op. cit.*, p. 266.

[7] Fals-Borda, *Peasant Society in the Colombian Andes*, p. 227.

[8] W. R. Inge, *Protestantism*, p. 3.

[9] J. E. McFadyen, *A Guide to the Understanding of the Old Testament*, p. 63.

[10] Inge *op. cit.*, p. 7.

[11] *Ibid.*, p. 6.

[12] *Ibid.*, pp. 7–8.

[13] Ray Freeman Jenney, *I Am a Protestant*, pp. 79 ff.

[14] *Ibid.*, p. 89.

[15] Julio Navarro Monzó, *The Religious Problem in Latin American Culture*, p. 87.

[16] Alfonso López Michelsen, *Cuestiones Colombianas* (reviewed in " El Problema Religioso en la Realidad Colombiana," *El Evangelista Colombiano*, May, 1955, p. 6).

[17] Father Francis J. Connell, *Freedom of Worship, the Catholic Position*, p. 10.

[18] John A. Mackay, *God's Order*, p. 184.

[19] Paul Tillich, *Dynamics of Faith*, p. 71.

[20] Mackay, *God's Order*, p. 185.

Chapter IX. Faith in Action

[1] In the year 1882, General Justo Rufino Barrios, President of Guatemala, in a meeting with the officers of the Board of Foreign Missions of the Presbyterian Church U.S.A, invited the Board to send missionaries to his country.

[2] *Christian Work in South America,* Montevideo Congress Report, Vol. III, p. 73.

[3] Reported in *The New York Times,* June 3, 1957.

[4] John A. Mackay, "Our Future as Protestants," *Presbyterian Life,* January 6, 1951.

[5] Father Albert J. Nevins, "How Catholic Is Latin America?", *The Sign,* September, 1956.

[6] *Ibid.*

[7] Paper on "The Practical Presentation of Our Message," read at the Latin American Evangelical Conference in Buenos Aires, July, 1949; unpublished manuscript.

[8] *The Responsible Society,* an ecumenical enquiry published by the Study Department of the World Council of Churches, 1949, p. 10.

[9] "Fraternal worker" is the term used with reference to a person who is sent by one church to work under another in a different country.

Bibliography

Agate, Leonard D., *Luther and the Reformation*. T. C. & E. C. Jack, Ltd., London, 1913.

Arciniegas, Germán, *Green Continent*. Alfred A. Knopf, Inc., 1944.

——, *The State of Latin America*. Alfred A. Knopf, Inc., 1952.

Argüedas, Alcides, *Pueblo Enfermo*. Editorial Ercilla, Santiago, Chile, 1937.

Azevedo, Fernando de, *Brazilian Culture*. The Macmillan Company, 1950.

Barbieri, Sante U., *Spiritual Currents in Spanish America*. La Aurora, Buenos Aires, 1951.

Barros Hurtado, César, *América — Penurias de Libertad*. (Published by the author), Buenos Aires, 1950.

Barth, Karl, *The Epistle to the Romans*. Oxford University Press, London, 1933.

Benavente, Fray Toribio de (Motolinía), *Relaciones de la Nueva España*. Universidad Nacional Autónoma, Mexico, 1956.

Brenner, Anita, *Idols Behind Altars*. Harcourt, Brace and Company, Inc., 1929.

Bunge, Carlos Octavio, *Nuestra América*. Casa Vaccaro, Buenos Aires, 1918.

Castro, Américo, *The Structure of Spanish History*. Princeton University Press, 1954.

Collier, John, and Buitrón, Aníbal, *The Awakening Valley*. University of Chicago Press, 1949.

Connell, Francis J., *Freedom of Worship, the Catholic Position*. The Paulist Press, 1944.

David, F. D., *Our Neighbors of the Andes*. Field Afar Press, Catholic Foreign Mission Society, 1947.

Delpech, Jacques, *The Oppression of Protestants in Spain*. The Beacon Press, Inc., 1955.

Diffie, Bailey W., *Latin American Civilization*. Stackpole Sons, 1943.

Dostoevsky, Fyodor, *The Brothers Karamazov*. Random House Inc., (undated).

Espy, Willard R., *Bold New Program*. Bantam Books, Inc., 1950.

Fals-Borda, Orlando, *Peasant Society in the Colombian Andes*. University of Florida Press, 1955.

Frank, Waldo, *South of Us*. Garden City Books, 1940.

Freyre, Gilberto, *Brazil, an Interpretation*. Alfred A. Knopf, Inc., 1945.

Goslin, Thomas S., *Los Evangélicos en la América Latina*. La Aurora, Buenos Aires, 1956.

Gutiérrez Marín, Claudio, *Historia de la Reforma en España*. Casa Unida de Publicaciones, Mexico, 1942.

Hanke, Lewis, *Bartolomé de las Casas — Historian*. University of Florida Press, 1952.

———, *Bartolomé de las Casas — Pensador Político, Historiador, Antropólogo*. Sociedad Económica de Amigos del País, Havana, Cuba, 1949.

Haring, Clarence H., *The Spanish American Empire*. Oxford University Press, 1947.

Herring, Hubert, *A History of Latin America*. Alfred A. Knopf, Inc., 1955.

Howard, George P., *We Americans North and South*. Friendship Press, 1951.

Igne, W. R., *Protestantism*. Ernest Benn, Ltd., London, 1928.

———, *The Church in the World*. Longmans, Green & Co., Ltd., London, 1927.

Inman, Samuel Guy, *Latin America, Its Place in World Life*. Willett, Clark & Company, 1937.

Jenks, David, *Six Great Missionaries of the Sixteenth–Seventeenth Centuries*. A. R. Mowbray & Company, Ltd., London, 1930.

Jenney, Ray Freeman, *I Am a Protestant*. The Bobbs-Merrill Company, Inc., 1951.

Kraemer, Hendrik, *Religion and the Christian Faith*. The Westminster Press, 1956.

Latourette, Kenneth S., *Desafío a Los Protestantes*. La Aurora, Buenos Aires, 1957.

Lee, Elizabeth M., *He Wears Orchids*. Friendship Press, 1951.

Lewis, Oscar, *Life in a Mexican Village*. University of Florida Press, 1951.

Lockwood, Agnese, *Indians of the Andes*. Carnegie Endowment for International Peace, 1956.

López Michelsen, Alfonso, *La Estirpe Calvinista de Nuestras Instituciones*. Universidad Nacional de Colombia, Bogotá, 1947.

Mackay, John A., *The Other Spanish Christ*. The Macmillan Company, 1932.

———, *God's Order*. The Macmillan Company, 1953.

Madariaga, Salvador de, *Englishmen, Frenchmen and Spaniards*. Oxford University Press, London, 1928.

———, *The Rise of the Spanish American Empire*. The Macmillan Company, 1947.

———, *The Fall of the Spanish American Empire*. The Macmillan Company, 1947.

McFadyen, J. E., *A Guide to the Understanding of the Old Testament*. James Clarke & Company, Ltd., 1927.

Moog, Vianna, *Bandeirantes e Pioneiros, Paralelo Entre Duas Culturas*. Editora Globo, Rio de Janeiro, 1954.

Moses, Bernard, *South America on the Eve of Emancipation*. G. P. Putnam's Sons, London, 1908.

Navarro Monzó, Julio, *The Religious Problem in Latin American Culture*, English translation from the Spanish edition. Published by the Young Men's Christian Association, 1925.

———, *Los Conceptos que de Cristo Tiene la América Latina*. Imprenta Kidd, Buenos Aires, 1930.

Nóbrega, Manoel da, *Demagogia Política e Religiosa*. Recife, Brazil, 1955.

Otero, Gustavo Adolfo, *Figura y Carácter del Indio*. (Published by the author), Bolivia.

Pattee, Richard, *Catholicism in Latin America*. National Catholic Welfare Conference, Washington, 1945.

Picón y Salas, Mariano, *De la Conquista a la Independencia*. Fondo de Cultura Económica, Buenos Aires, 1944.

Pierson, Donald, *Negroes in Brazil*. University of Chicago Press, 1942.

Prescott, W. H., *Conquest of Peru*. Hurst and Co. (undated).

Quintanilla, Luis, *A Latin American Speaks*. The Macmillan Company, 1943.

Rojas, Ricardo, *The Invisible Christ*. Abingdon Press, 1931.

Rycroft, W. Stanley, ed., *Indians of the High Andes*. Committee on Cooperation in Latin America, 1946.

Schurz, William Lytle, *This New World*. E. P. Dutton & Co., Inc., 1954.

Sterling, Mathew, *Indians of the Americas*. National Geographic Society, 1955.

Stubbs, William M., *How Europe Was Won for Christianity*. Fleming H. Revell Company, 1913.

Tannenbaum, Frank, *Peace by Revolution*. Columbia University Press, 1933.

Tawney, R. H., *Religion and the Rise of Capitalism*. Penguin Books Ltd., London, 1938.

Thomas, A. B., *Latin America, a History*. The Macmillan Company, 1956.

Tillich, Paul, *Dynamics of Faith*. Harper & Bros., 1957.

Vaillant, G. C., *The Aztecs of Mexico*. Penguin Books Ltd., London, 1950.

Verissimo, Erico, *Brazilian Literature*. The Macmillan Company, 1945.

Zavala, Silvio, *New Viewpoints on the Spanish Colonization of America*. University of Pennsylvania Press, 1943.

PERIODICALS, BULLETINS, AND REPORTS

Baez Camargo, Gonzalo, "A Roman Catholic Revival," *Christianity and Crisis,* September 29, 1952.

Chase Manhattan Bank, *Latin American Business Highlights,* September, 1955.

Christopher, Robert Allen, "The Human Race in Brazil," *Américas,* Vol. 5, No. 7, July, 1953. Pan American Union Washington, D.C.

Inman, Samuel Guy, "The Impact of the Modern World on Latin America — a Politico-Economic and Technological Approach," *Civilisations* (Quarterly), Vol. V (1955), No. 4.

López Michelsen, Alfonso, *Cuestiones Colombianas,* reviewed in "El Problema Religioso en la Realidad Colombiana," *El Evangelista Colombiano,* May, 1955.

Mackay, John A., "Our Future as Protestants," *Presbyterian Life,* January 6, 1951.

Maryknoll Fathers, *Proceedings of the Lima Methods Conference of the Maryknoll Fathers.*

Montevideo Congress Report, *Christian Work in South America,* Vol. III. Committee on Cooperation in Latin America, 1925.

Nevins, Albert J., "How Catholic Is Latin America?", *The Sign,* September, 1956.

Northrop, F. S. C., "The Struggle for Order and Progress," *Civilisations* (Quarterly), Vol. V (1955), No. 4.

Pattee, Richard, "The Apostasy of the Masses," *The Holy Name Journal,* November 11, 1945.

Rembao, Alberto, "Pre-Hispanic Religion in Modern Mexico," *International Review of Missions,* April, 1942.

United Nations, *Population of South America, 1950–80,* and *Population of Central America, 1950–80.* Bureau of Social Affairs, Population Branch, 1955.

Vela, J. Bort, "When Least Expected," *Ibérica,* July 15, 1956.

Glossary

abrazo — embrace

aires — literally means "air currents," but has reference to maleficent effects of these on people

ayllu — village community among the Inca people of Peru

Altiplano — high plateau (Bolivia)

bandeirantes — frontiersmen in early Brazilian history

Candomblé — Afro-Brazilian fetish cult

casas grandes — big houses or mansions of Brazilian planters in colonial period

caudillo — chieftain, leader, especially in political struggle

caudillismo — leadership of strong man in politics

chásquis — runners in relays among the Inca people

chicha — fermented drink made from corn

chocolatl — Aztec word for chocolate

conquistador — conqueror

criollo — creole, indigenous

cura — priest

curacas — headmen among Inca people

dignidad — dignity

encomendero — Spanish colonist who benefited by encomienda system

encomienda — institution that gave early Spanish colonists the right to demand services and collect tribute from conquered Indian people

fiestas — festivities, holidays

fiesta brava — bullfight

Fuero Juzgo — compilation of Visigoth common law, introduced into Spain in the 5th and the 6th centuries

Gaucho — herdsman of the Argentine pampas

guano — bird-dropping fertilizer

hacendado — planter, landowner

huacas — Indian burial grounds (Peru)

honor — honor

latifundistas — large landowners

llanos — plains (Venezuela)

mañana — morning, tomorrow

mantilla — veil or head shawl

mestizo — half-breed

padre — father, priest

pampas — extensive plains (Argentina)

peones — day laborers

plaza — town square

política criolla — local politics, usually characterized by intrigue

pulque — fermented juice of the maguey plant

quena — Indian flute (Peru)

reducciones — settlements of Indians converted by the Spaniards

requerimiento — legal notice or intimation

seitas — sects or religious groups

senzalas — slave quarters on sugar plantations in colonial Brazil

sierra — mountain range

tamales — Mexican dish of highly seasoned, crushed maize and meat

teocallis — Aztec temples

tortillas — thin unleavened pancakes (Mexico)

tunal — prickly pear bush

yerba mate — tea made from herbs (Argentina and Paraguay)

Index